THE MARATHONERS

BY HAL HIGDON

G. P. Putnam's Sons · New York

Special thanks to Kevin Shyne for his assistance in compiling the information on the ten great marathoners of all time.

Library of Congress Cataloging in Publication Data
Higdon, Hal.
  The marathoners.
  Includes index.
  SUMMARY: Includes biographies stressing the achievements of some outstanding marathon runners of modern times and describes the major marathon events around the world.
    1. Runners (Sports)—Biography—Juvenile literature.
2. Marathon running—Juvenile literature. [1. Runners (Sports) 2. Marathon running] I. Title.
GV697.A1H5165   1980   796.4′26′0922 [B] [920]   80-10469
ISBN 0-399-20695-7

CONTENTS

THE MARATHONERS

1
BREAK POINT

There is a moment in every marathon referred to as the break point. It is the moment the race will be won—or lost. It is the moment one runner, or sometimes a group of runners, breaks away from the others in the field.

"Often the Japanese will run under control for mile after mile waiting for that exact moment," says Frank Shorter, "the time to make their break."

In December, 1971, Frank Shorter, a law student at the University of Florida, won the Fukuoka Marathon in Japan, one of the great races in the world over the classic marathon distance of 26 miles 385 yards. At Fukuoka, Frank ran 2:12:50.4, a time close to the Olympic record of 2:12:11, set by Ethiopia's Abebe Bikila in Tokyo in 1964. In that key Japanese race, Frank also defeated some of the top marathoners in the world: John Farrington of Australia, Jack Foster of New Zealand, Akio Usami of Japan.

Frank, however, does not like to talk about defeating other runners. He said after that race, "I finished and a great feeling of thankfulness swept through me. There was no sense of conquest, none of this baloney about *vanquishing* anybody." As soon as he crossed the line he turned to embrace Usami, who finished a half minute behind him. "My only thought," said Frank, "was 'we made it.' This man had suffered as much as I."

Because of his Fukuoka victory, when Frank Shorter arrived in Munich, Germany, the following summer for the 1972 Olympic Games, he was ranked as one of the favorites to win the marathon. The experts favored Frank even though he would be running only his fifth race in an event where experience counts. He was a favorite even though no American had won the Olympic marathon since 1908 in London when Johnny Hayes of New York won a disputed victory.

In that 1908 race, the Italian Dorando Pietri had surged into the lead past Charles Hefferon with only two miles to go. He came into the stadium more than a minute ahead of Hayes, who also had passed Hefferon. But the Italian was staggering from fatigue and the heat. He started the wrong way around the track, and when he discovered his mistake, fell down.

The officials picked him up, but he fell again. And twice again. Finally the officials half carried Dorando Pietri across the line, and watched as the American Johnny Hayes came in second. But the rules state you must run without help, so Dorando Pietri was disqualified. Johnny Hayes was declared the winner in 2:55:18.4.

Ironically, Dorando Pietri might have won the race had it been the same distance of 24½ miles as the first marathon at the Olympic Games in Greece in 1896. This marathon was held in memory of a run by the lengendary Pheidippides from the plains of Marathon into Athens to announce the Athenian victory over the Persians. Marathons at succeeding Olympic Games (Paris in 1900, St. Louis in 1904) covered similar distances.

But at London in 1908, Olympic officials wanted to begin the race at Windsor Castle, supposedly so the grandchildren of King Edward VII and Queen Alexandra could see the start. The distance between the castle and the finish line at the Olympic Stadium outside London was 26 miles 385 yards. So Dorando Pietri had collapsed only after having run roughly a mile farther than any other Olympic marathoner before him.

Because of that 1908 Olympic race, the official marathon distance everywhere has been set at 26 miles 385 yards—or 42.195 kilometers. The list of great marathoners to follow the footsteps of Pietri (and Pheidippides) included such men as Hannes Kolehmainen of Finland, winner of the 10,000 and 5,000 meters at Stockholm in 1912, who came back after World War I to win the marathon in Antwerp in 1920, Emil Zatopek of Czechoslovakia, who in the 1952 Olympics at Helsinki won not only those two track events, but also the marathon, and an unknown Ethiopian named Abebe Bikila, who appeared at Rome in 1960 and won the marathon running barefoot over hard-surfaced roads. To prove it was not a fluke, Bikila repeated his victory at Tokyo four years later, becoming the only athlete to win two Olympic marathons.

During this period the United States had many fine marathon runners, but none quite good enough to challenge for the Olympic gold medal. Clarence DeMar won the famed Boston Marathon seven times over a span of 19 years, but the best he ran in the Olympics was third in 1924. John A. Kelley won Boston twice in 1935 and 1945, and John J. Kelley (no relation) won the same race in 1957 and finished second on five occasions. But neither did well in the Olympics.

During the mid-1960's, America's Buddy Edelen ranked among the top marathoners in the world. He won the Kosice Marathon in Czechoslovakia in 1963, running 2:15:09.6. He might have challenged Bikila at Tokyo, but the American Olympic trials the following year which were run in 96-degree heat, sapped his energy and although he won, he never quite recovered. Later that summer he finished sixth at Tokyo—a good performance, but not a gold-winning one.

In 1972 at Munich, however, Frank Shorter appeared to have the best chance of any American since Johnny Hayes to win the gold medal in the Olympic marathon. In the four years since the previous Olympic Games in Mexico, Frank had emerged as one of the top track runners in the world at distances from two miles to 10,000 meters (just over six miles). Five days before the marathon at Munich, he placed fifth in the 10,000 meters, running 27:51.4, only a straightaway behind Lasse Viren of Finland who ran a 27:38.4 world record. It was obvious Frank Shorter possessed good speed.

He also had good endurance. Frank could go the distance. He trained by running 150 miles a week. Only fifteen months prior to his Munich race, Frank ran his first marathon in Eugene, Oregon, coming in second behind Kenny Moore and qualifying to run the Pan American Games Marathon in Columbia later that summer. He won the gold medal in Columbia and then took the race in December at Fukuoka.

Frank Shorter was tough. He had drive. He also had great confidence in his ability to succeed, almost to the point of cockiness. He wanted to win.

At Munich on the morning of September 10, 1972, he arose early. He did not go out to run as he normally does. Like most world-class distance runners, Frank trains twice a day, once in the morning and once in the afternoon. The only time he does not train twice daily is the day of a marathon. "The marathon is a long distance," he says. "Any steps you take that day are too many, if you don't take them toward the finish line."

He ate a breakfast that included cereal and pancakes. An hour before the race Frank left the Olympic Village to go to the stadium. Other runners were there, some of them resting, some of them warming up. Among them were Britain's Ron Hill, Belgium's Karel Lismont, the European champion, Ethiopia's Mamu Wolde, the defending Olympic champion, Belgium's Gaston Roelants, who had won a gold medal in the steeplechase (a 3,000 meter Olympic track event with four hurdles and one water jump per lap) four years before, and Australia's Derek Clayton, holder of the world's fastest marathon time of 2:08:33.*

Frank studied the men he would have to run against. He looked for signs of weakness. He could learn little. He decided to jog a mile to warm up. Then he changed to the shirt he would wear in the race, a white vest with USA on the front in blue letters lined with red. Sewed on front and back was the number 1014 by which officials and spectators could identify him.

He went into the stadium to wait for the start.

*Clayton ran 2:08:33 in 1969 over a course in Belgium that was never accurately measured.

2
"EVEN THE OLYMPICS"

Few residents of the Olympic city who would watch
Frank Shorter run that day probably realized that the
slender American with short-cropped black hair and a
bushy mustache beneath a hooked nose had, like many of
them, been born in Munich. The date was October 31,
1947. It was soon after World War II and his father, a
doctor, was stationed with the U.S. Army in Germany at
the time. Frank was the second of nine children; he has
seven sisters.

His father soon completed his army service and
moved back to the United States, practicing in
Middletown, New York, where Frank grew up. Frank
began running in 1963 at the age of fifteen while attending Mount Hermon, a prep school.

Frank started running mainly to get in shape for
skiing. He competed in downhill, jumping, and cross-
country, and had as his boyhood heroes not famous
ballplayers, or even runners, but famous skiers of the era:
François Bonlieu, André Duvillard, Guy Perillat, and
André Molterer (Austrian silver medalist in the 1956
Olympics).

During the fall, as part of his pre-ski conditioning
program, he entered a local 4.33-mile running event, the
Bemus Pie Race, which is the oldest continuously run race

14

in the country, older than even the Boston Marathon. Frank finished seventh in the 4.33 mile race, beaten only by the five members of the Mount Herman cross-country team (who that year had won the New England prep league cross-country title) and another skier who had been the National Junior Nordic combined champion (jumping and running). "I must be able to do something good," thought Frank, so the next spring he went out for track.

As a sophomore, he ran 4:45 for the mile and 10:02 for two miles, but halfway through the season decided to play baseball instead. He batted .380 for the junior varsity. That fall he appeared for cross-country practice. The first day, the coach had the team run the 2.5-mile course, and it turned into a race. Frank finished fifth among the nearly eighty team candidates. By the end of the season he was running second behind George Bowman, who won the New England cross-country championship. In his senior year, Frank won the New England cross-country championship and ran 4:30 and 9:38 in track. He also ranked third in studies in his class and enrolled at Yale University.

During his first three years at Yale, Frank competed on the cross-country and track teams, but did not take running very seriously. He had many other interests. He studied to maintain high grades because he expected to go to medical school and become a doctor like his father. During the winter he skied. Often after an indoor winter track meet on Saturday, Frank would head for Vermont with friends the following day to go skiing. When the track team traveled to Florida on its annual spring vacation trip, Frank did not accompany them. He preferred to tour with a Yale singing group known as The Bachelors. Frank failed to place in the two-mile in the crucial dual meet between Harvard and Yale. In his junior year he ran 9:05, which was good enough only for fourth place.

The year was 1968. Before leaving for summer vacation, Frank stopped by the office of Yale track coach Bob Giegengack to talk about his future. Giegengack was also one of the American Olympic coaches. He was leaving soon for the Olympic track team's training camp at Lake Tahoe, California.

"Frank, if you ever got serious about your running," Giegengack told the young runner, "there would be no limit to what you could do."

"Even the Olympics?" suggested Frank.

"Even the Olympics," said his coach.

Giegengack advised Shorter to train harder during the summer. He wanted him to increase his mileage. "Come back here your senior year and do your distance work in the morning, your quality work in the afternoon, and we'll see what happens."

Frank planned to spend that summer in Taos, New Mexico, where his father was then practicing medicine. Taos was not far from Alamosa, Colorado, where the trials to pick the three runners representing the United States in the 1968 Olympic marathon were scheduled for August. The Yale coach suggested that Frank consider running in those marathon trials, if only for experience. He felt that Frank's light build, smooth stride, and strong endurance might make him better adapted to the marathon than any of the shorter track distances.

Frank did not try the 1968 Olympic trials, but he did run all summer long. And he improved. In the fall he returned to school and placed 18th in the NCAA cross-country championships, a standing good enough to earn him All-American honors. At the NCAA indoor track championships, he showed even more improvement, placing second with 8:45.2.

That spring he ran the mile in 4:06.4, a time which remains his best only because he later rarely had a chance

16

to run a mile in top competition. At the NCAA outdoor track meet he placed second in the three-mile (13:43.4) and first in the six-mile (29:00.2). The times, however, were less important than the top places.

Frank also placed fourth in the six-mile at the AAU track championships (28:52.0) and earned a trip to Europe to compete in dual track meets against West Germany and Great Britain. He placed third and fourth in four-man fields. His time against the British was 29:16.4 for 10,000 meters. (Since it takes about one minute more to run 10,000 meters than six miles, this was his best time for the distance by quite a bit.*)

Though outclassed when running against more experienced international athletes, Frank Shorter began to get a feel for what he might accomplish if he began to take his running more seriously.

He returned home and went to medical school at the University of New Mexico, as planned. But his taste of glory caused him to rethink his goals. Four years ahead were the 1972 Olympics in Munich, Germany. But also ahead were four years of difficult studies to earn an M.D. degree. Frank realized that he had to choose between the goal of becoming a doctor and the goal of fulfilling his abilities as an athlete. He chose the latter course, and two months later dropped out of medical school.

He did not abandon school entirely, however; he simply shifted courses. The Yale track team had competed in the Florida Relays the previous spring, and Frank had gotten to know some of the runners who ran there. The city of Gainesville, Florida, had become something of a mecca for budding distance runners, due to the presence of Jack Bacheler, a graduate student at the university who had qualified for the finals in the 5,000 meters at the 1968

*The 10,000 meter run is 376 yards farther than the six-mile.

17

Olympics.

Frank later explained to writer Joe Henderson the reason for the Gainesville move: "Many people I have met have the 'if-onlys.' *If only* I could train harder, would I be good.' I just decided that I'd see how good I could get in a few months. I also started out with the realization that things might not go too well. But at least I wouldn't have the 'if-onlys.' "

In Florida, Frank Shorter did not train often with Bacheler, because their schedules differed. Jack usually ran at six-thirty in the morning with a group. Frank had late classes and liked to sleep. But when he did wake up, he trained hard, running usually eight or ten miles in the morning at a pace between 6:30 and 7:00 per mile.

In the afternoon he would run a second workout, often at the University of Florida quarter mile (440-yard) track. A typical workout Frank did at this time was to run 20 × 440, jogging a quick 110 between each quarter to recover. He ran these at a speed of near 65 seconds. Within a period of a few months during the spring of 1970, he tripled the amount of miles he ran each week to nearly 150.

Together, Bacheler and Shorter soon ranked as the top two distance runners in America, finishing one-two or often tying for first in many of the races they ran.

At the National AAU outdoor track meet in 1970, Frank won the three-mile in 13:24.2 and tied with Jack in the six-mile at 27:24.0. He won the 10,000-meter against the Russians that summer in 28:22.8. *Track & Field News* ranked Frank second in the world in that event for 1970. Frank also won a major 12-mile road race (the Springbank International) in London, Ontario, the AAU cross-country race in Chicago, and Sao Silvestre, a major road run of 4.5 miles held each New Year's Eve in São Paulo, Brazil.

18

Frank Shorter began to think ahead to competing in the Olympic Games in 1972. Everyone, including Frank himself, now assumed he would qualify for the American team. But the question was: what event or which events would he run? On February 19, 1971, he set an American record for the two-mile indoors with a time of 8:26.2, but there was no Olympic two-mile. His best success outdoors seemed to come at 10,000 meters, the metric equal to the six-mile run. But Kenny Moore, an Olympic competitor in the marathon in 1968, suggested that Frank join him in the marathon. "You've got the speed," suggested Kenny, "and you know you can go the distance."

Roy Benson, the distance coach at the University of Florida, had watched Shorter develop. He commented: "It's almost automatic that people who train at Frank's level—about 150 miles a week—try the marathon. For them, it's just a long training run. They're running 20 miles in training workouts enough of the time, so that finishing a marathon is no big deal."

The 1971 Pan American Games were to take place in Cali, Colombia, in August. Like the Olympics, the Pan Am Games occur every four years, but, unlike the Olympics, include only countries in the half of the world occupied by the Americas. Frank decided to test his marathoning ability in the Pan Am Games, but first he had to qualify for the team by placing first or second in the AAU marathon championships in Eugene, Oregon, on Sunday, June 6. Frank had little money at that time, so in order to get to the West Coast he accepted an invitation to compete in the Kennedy Games in Berkeley, California, on Saturday, only the day before. He ran three miles in 13:31, then headed north to Eugene.

Frank ran with a pack of other runners for the first 13 miles of the 26-mile marathon race, and then began to force the pace. Only Kenny Moore and John Vitale of

19

Connecticut stayed with him, and Vitale soon faded. With three miles left, Moore pulled away, winning in 2:16:48.6. "I really dragged the last two miles," recalls Frank. But he finished second in his first marathon in 2:17:44.6, a time which qualified him for the Pan Am team.

Later, Frank commented to writer Lawrence Shainberg of the *New York Times Magazine* concerning his defeat by Moore: "He finished one minute ahead of me, but I knew then he'd never do it again."

Frank Shorter was not being cocky; he was making a simple statement of fact. He also has said about the marathon, "I don't consider coming in second losing. It's just not winning."

At the Pan American Games Frank qualified at 10,000 meters and won that event early in the week with a time of 28:50.8. But between the 10,000 and the marathon, he became sick with diarrhea.

At five miles into the marathon Frank started to get goose bumps. "I knew I was going to be in trouble," Frank commented later. Finally at 16 miles, he ran off the road and into a drainage ditch for what runners often refer to as a "pit stop."

Frank quickly returned to the race, having been passed by only one Mexican runner, José Gaspar. Several hundred yards farther ahead were the leaders he had been running with: Kenny Moore, Alvaro Mejia of Colombia (winner of the 1971 Boston Marathon), and another Colombian, Herman Barreneche.

Frank knew he couldn't win, but he hoped to recover quickly enough to earn at least one of the medals awarded to the top three finishers. He soon passed Gaspar and within several miles was back with the leaders. He moved up silently behind them and finally said: "Yoo hoo. I'm back."

Kenny Moore turned around, shocked at Shorter's

sudden appearance. Mejia grimaced. The ease with which he caught them seemed to demoralize the other runners. Frank won in 2:22:40 after Kenny dropped out of the race from the heat.

It was then that Frank Shorter realized his best chance for success in the Munich Olympics the following year would be the marathon. Although he still planned to run the 10,000 meters and hoped to do well, he began to look forward to his greatest success being in the Olympic Games' longest-running race.

3
RUNNING FAST

The 1972 marathon race would begin and end on the red, rubberized track of the main Olympic stadium. In between, it would wind on a twisting course through the streets of Munich. A few stretches followed gravel paths through parks.

When the gun sounded, Frank moved into the lead, mainly because nobody else wanted it. He ran the first 400 meters around the track in the stadium in 72 seconds, and after being passed, went the next 800 meters in 2:24. His 4:48-per-mile pace, if held over the full 26-mile distance, would result in a world and Olympic record.

But once out of sight of the 80,000 spectators in the main stadium, the marathoners slowed their pace, aware that the early leader rarely wins the race. They flowed through the marathon gate under the stadium and out onto the streets of Munich. They followed a square truck with a revolving red light. People lined the streets, applauding the runners as they passed.

Clayton and Hill pushed to the front; Shorter seemed content to remain one of the lead pack of several dozen runners who drew farther and farther ahead of the slower runners among the small field. (Only 62 would finish the race.) Each country could enter only its three

22

fastest men. Even the "slower" runners were fast enough to win most races run in their own country. Yet they were seeing their chance at an Olympic medal vanish down the road ahead of them.

The lead runners passed five kilometers in 15:51. Five kilometers (5,000 meters) is a few hundred yards farther than three miles, about 30 seconds more. So 15:51 translated to about 5:10-per-mile, a relatively slow pace for such an elite field. Despite the slow pace, Frank felt poorly. "For some reason we were really dragging," he said later. "And I didn't feel that good." Later, he would realize he felt bad *because* the pace was so slow.

Frank ran easily between ten and 15 kilometers. At about that point the pace seemed to slow again. Clayton and Hill started to drop back, and Akio Usami of Japan and Jack Foster of New Zealand moved ahead. Only eight runners remained together in the lead pack, but clusters of other runners were close behind. The winner that day still might be among them.

It was still early in the race. Two-thirds of the course lay ahead of the runners. Nearly 17 miles remained to be run. But Frank Shorter decided to make his move.

Frank later told John Parker (author of *The Frank Shorter Story*): "I decided that, rather than slow down with the pack, I would let my momentum carry me to the front. So I just let it go and got a ten-yard lead very easily. I ran a little harder, and no one came with me. I pushed a little more, and still no one. So I thought, 'Okay, I guess this will be it.' "

The 1972 Olympic marathon had reached its break point. Or had it? There were still 17 miles to run. The question remained: could Frank Shorter hold the lead gained with such apparent ease?

Kenny Moore, another American in the Olympic marathon, seemed stunned by Frank's move so early in

23

the race. He was equally surprised that none of the other runners accepted the challenge. "Nobody went with him," Kenny later wrote in *Sports Illustrated*. "It was hot and it seemed he had spurted too sharply. He would pay for his extravagance later. So as he moved away, we each sought our most economic rhythm, and the pack split up."

Frank Shorter pressed hard for the next five kilometers, opening up a lead of 31 seconds on the runners behind him. He had run the first five kilometers of the race at a 5:10 pace. Now as he passed 20 kilometers in 1:01:30, he estimated that his pace had quickened over the following 15 kilometers to near 4:50 per mile. At certain points, when he made his break, he was moving faster, perhaps close to 4:40.

As an example of the speed at which Frank Shorter was moving in the 1972 Olympic marathon, a runner who can run even a single mile near 4:40 can win many high school track races. Frank was running that fast in the middle of a 26-mile race!

"I just ran as hard as I could," Frank commented later, "and no one came up on me. In the middle of the race I don't remember anything, except just trying to run as hard as I could within myself. That is, to push as fast as possible and still feel good. That's all I cared about. I forgot the runners behind me."

As Frank Shorter increased his lead in the marathon, he ran as though through a canyon of people. Only 80,000 could crowd into the main Olympic stadium to see the track and field events. Even most citizens of Munich, Germany, would have to depend on television for their view of the great athletic events within their home town. Tickets were expensive, as much as $20 a seat.

But one event was free: the marathon. Only the first half and the final quarter mile were within the Olympic stadium before paying customers. The rest of the

26-mile 385-yard course wound through the streets of Munich. People could see the marathon for free by finding a place to stand on the course and waiting for the runners to come past. They would see only a few minutes of a drama that would take more than two hours to complete, but at least they would feel that they had been part of the 1972 Olympic Games—even if only as spectators.

So spectators crowded onto each side of the course, sometimes as many as five and ten deep on the curb, and waited patiently for the runners. Some carried programs or newspapers that included a map of the course and a list of the runners entered. Soon there was a stir of excitement as the flashing, circular red light atop the electric truck leading the runners appeared off in the distance. There were other trucks, too, for reporters and photographers. The trucks were electric, since gasoline engines would cause polluting exhaust fumes which would be bad for the runners to breathe.

The trucks passed, and then the runners came in clusters, like swarms of bees, huddled together almost as though for their own protection. There was a single runner out front, then a cluster, then one or two runners alone, then another cluster, and another, and finally those who already had fallen behind in ones and twos. Near the end, all the runners would be strung out over several miles of the course, but in the early stages they still ran together.

Only a few of the spectators knew the identity of the runners passing them. They could tell which country many of the runners came from by the names or the flags on their shirts, but most spectators probably could not identify the runners by name. They did not know that the first runner to pass with USA across his chest was Shorter, or the second Moore, or the third Bacheler. They did not realize that the black runner with the green shirt was

25

Mamo Wolde of Ethiopia, who had won that same race in Mexico City four years before.

Even those familiar with the sport of long-distance running could not catch all the faces, numbers, and match them with the right names in their programs. At a speed of only 12 mph, the runners still passed too fast. But it was enough for the spectators to be part of a spectacle and to know that they were witnesses to the marathon which is considered, along with the ten-event decathlon, one of the most important events in the Olympic Games.

As the Olympic marathon continued, Frank Shorter ran smoothly, his feet seeming barely to brush the surface of the road. At 5 feet 11 inches and 130 pounds, Frank was slender, almost slight. A marathoner has little need for muscle—particularly upper body muscle—and he has *no* use for fat.

Most marathoners probably have a body-fat content of around 10%, half of what the average American might have. Anyone with more than 25% body fat is considered obese.* Frank Shorter's body fat is only 2.7%, very, very low, even for a long-distance runner.

Frank's most important muscles are those of his legs. His legs are sinewy, like those of a deer. They pumped rapidly as he propelled himself along the course.

His stride was short, but efficient. A distance runner does not take long, bounding strides, but instead many fast, short ones. You can only push yourself forward while your feet are on the ground. A long, bounding stride may look attractive, but it will not get you to the finish line first, particularly in a race 26 miles long. The marathoner must conserve every ounce of his energy and flow along the surface of the road, not picking his knees up any higher than necessary.

---

*Women usually have 5% more body fat than men, so values differ for them.

Frank's arms swung in rhythm to the movement of his legs. They were bent at the elbow at about a 90-degree angle. His hands were cupped slightly, brushing across the top of his dark blue, nylon running shorts. He also wore the white USA vest that all other members of the American Olympic track team wore in the games. Attached to it, front and back, was the same number (1014) that he had worn in the finals of the 10,000 meters five days before.

Before a race, Frank Shorter usually mutilates race numbers. He trims them, tearing off each last inch of white cardboard or cloth surrounding the black numeral itself. At the American Olympic trials two months earlier, he had cut his race number 43 in half, placing the "4" on one side of the Florida orange on the front of his shirt and the "3" on the other.

It is almost as though Frank wants to avoid carrying even the fraction of an ounce represented by the extra paper on his 26-mile trip. He also wants to avoid the number blocking any cooling breeze he might get on his shirt. But for the Olympics, Frank left his numbers intact.

Other than undershorts, the only other items that Frank Shorter wore were a pair of running shoes, white with black stripes on the side. They were lightweight with thin rubber bottoms. He wore no socks. But, as Frank does every day in practice, he had bound tape around his feet to support his weak metatarsal arches.

Frank's feet are his one weakness, if they could be called a weakness. In addition to having weak arches, he is slightly pigeon-toed, which causes him to shuffle ever so slightly. He scrapes the outside of his shoes. As a result, he often wears out a single pair of shoes within three weeks. Of course, during that three weeks of training, he may have covered some 400 miles in twice-daily workouts.

After running 11 kilometers, Frank noticed blisters forming on his feet. They were partly a result of his shoes

27

being new and having thin soles. But Frank quickly forgot about them. Blisters would not affect his performance that day, and wouldn't bother him until after the race, so there was no sense worrying about them.

The reporters who write about the marathon (at least those reporters who do not run themselves) talk often about pain as though it is something a marathoner must endure constantly for 26 miles. Blisters, of course, can be one source of pain.

But a well-trained distance runner like Frank Shorter does not think about pain. He may not even feel it. For someone capable of running one mile near 4:00 pace (as Frank can), it is not painful to run nearly one minute per mile slower. Running at a 5:00 pace does not result in pain for a well-trained marathoner.

Pain is standing at the plate with a bat in your hand and being struck by a pitch thrown at 100 mph. Pain is throwing a forward pass and getting buried beneath a 250-pound lineman. Pain is jumping for a rebound and feeling an elbow thrown into your stomach. Pain is sudden and sharp. Such pain does not exist in a marathon, despite what reporters who cover these other sports think.

What does exist in a marathon is discomfort. And fatigue. And the feeling that you are not having a very good day. And the feeling that you have been running a long, long time.

Discomfort can be caused by many things: uncomfortable shoes, clothing that chafes the body, a hot sun that causes body temperature to rise, muscle cramps, and stiffness. On hilly courses runners sometimes must force their muscles to propel them up one side of a steep hill, then fight the pounding as they are carried too fast down the other side.

Fatigue comes upon a marathoner gradually, and

usually only when he is well into a race. Although it is not painful for a 4:00 miler to run a single mile in 5:00, the running of mile after mile at that pace causes fatigue. If the runner has gone too fast too soon, he becomes tired and often reaches a point where he must slow down or even stop. Marathoners sometimes refer to this as "hitting the wall." It often happens around 20 miles in a 26-mile race.

But as Frank ground steadily toward the finish line, he seemed strong enough to banish fatigue and crash through any wall that existed as though it were paper, not bricks.

As for feeling that he had been running a long, long time, Frank *had* been running a long time—for nine years since he first went out for track in high school. He had run twice-a-day workouts averaging 140 miles a week. It was because of all this running that Frank Shorter gradually was pulling away in the race from the others who hoped to win the gold medal that day.

Frank did not worry about pain, discomfort, or fatigue. Instead, he focused on the art of running. He concentrated on putting one foot in front of the other as smoothly and with as little effort as he could. Then he brought the rear foot up equally as smoothly.

A marathoner's foot touches the ground perhaps as often as three times a second. It takes maybe 1,000 foot-falls to cover a single mile. Multiply that by 26 for the full length of the marathon. The slower runners in long-distance races sometimes allow their minds to wander. They sometimes purposely think about other things to relieve the boredom of running for three or four hours non-stop.

But the top runners focus their minds on the act of running. They concentrate on maintaining balance, on swinging their arms properly, on keeping their knees low, on holding a smooth stride, on breathing in rhythm. Frank takes three steps for each breath in, three more for each breath out. The ability of some people to concentrate is one reason why they are superior runners.

This is true in other sports as well. The single most important trait common in all sports, other than raw talent, is an ability to concentrate. You must have talent or you will not succeed. But you also must *concentrate* on what you are doing. The batter must rivet his attention on the pitcher and the ball after it is thrown toward him. The golfer must focus his energy on swinging smoothly, then following through after he hits the ball. A race driver in the Indianapolis 500 coming into a turn must swing his steering wheel at the precise instant if he is to maintain maximum speed—and make that movement lap after lap. Concentration is vital in all sports.

Concentration was vital to Frank Shorter running in the Olympic marathon as well. Between 15 and 25 kilometers (a distance of six miles) he focused on the road before him, making certain that each step taken on it was as smooth and effortless as the last. Afterwards, he remembered almost nothing about those six miles other than that he had run—and run fast.

And he drank. Earlier that morning he had poured Coca-Cola into plastic bottles marked with his name. The Coke was defizzed, shaken to release its carbonation. Frank brought these bottles to the starting line, where race officials transferred them to refreshment points every few kilometers along the course.

But when the lead runners arrived at the first refreshment point at seven kilometers, an Ethiopian (not Wolde) running ahead of Frank took the bottle with Frank's name on it by mistake. Frank sprinted the 15 yards separating him from the Ethiopian and grabbed the

30

bottle from his hand. "That's mine!" he said, and drank from it.

Later at 25 kilometers, Frank's wife Louise awaited him before the refreshment point. She yelled that there was nothing with his name on it on the table. Since Frank was running in the lead, he knew it was the officials' mistake. Frank grabbed for water instead.

Most marathoners drink on the run. The hotter the day, the more they drink. They do this because on warm days they sweat more. The body sweats in order to cool itself. The moisture on the skin evaporates and this lowers body temperature. But the more a person sweats, the more water he loses. He becomes dehydrated.

Heat is the great enemy of long-distance runners. If body heat rises too high, the runner must slow down. It is like a high fever caused by sickness. If the runner fails to slow down and his body heat rises too high, he may suffer heat prostration and collapse. Runners may become so overheated on hot days that they could die if they fail to slow down or cool themselves.

So runners drink on hot days, as they run, to avoid dehydration. Every few miles in a marathon, they reach a refreshment table and grab water or other replacement fluids such as Gatorade, ERG (for electrolytic replacement glucose), or, as in the case of Frank Shorter, defizzed Coke. No matter how fast or how much they drink, however, they cannot equal the liquid their system loses through sweat as they run. But they drink, usually without even breaking stride, to try and stay cool.

Frank Shorter drank for yet another reason. He hoped that the high sugar content in the defizzed Coke would provide him with more energy. It might, and it might not. Scientists claim that drinks with too much sugar enter the bloodstream more slowly than ordinary water. But runners do not always listen to the scientists. They

31

listen to their bodies. And whether right or wrong, Frank felt that defizzed Coke worked best for him.

Among world-class marathoners, he seems to have less trouble on hot days than many of his rivals. It is partly because of his low (2.7 percent) body fat content. He is built for running in the heat. Because of this, he also gets cold easily on days when it is not warm. Even when the temperature is in the sixties, Frank often trains wearing a jacket and a wool cap.

On this day in Munich it was warm: in the mid-seventies. Frank Shorter continued to pull away from the runners behind him. In most international races runners receive times every five kilometers. Frank passed the first five-kilometer mark in 15:51 among the lead group of 26 runners. He went by ten kilometers in 31:24 (having run the second five kilometers in 15:33). He was then in 11th place, nine seconds behind Clayton and Hill.

He reached 15 kilometers in 46:21, covering the third five kilometers in 14:57, his fastest split during the race. At that point he had a five-second lead over a group of seven runners. Five seconds is nothing in a marathon race: 30 or 40 yards. A lead that small can be lost almost instantly. But Frank already had begun to pull away.

He passed 20 kilometers in 1:01:30, still pressing the pace, having run his fourth five-kilometer section in 15:09. Now he had a 31-second lead over Karel Lismont of Belgium. At 25 kilometers in 1:17:05 (15:35), he led by 53 seconds over Wolde, Moore, and Clayton. By 30 kilometers in 1:32:49 (15:44), his lead had increased to 1:05 over Wolde and Moore.

By now Frank's pace had slowed to where he ran at slower than 5:00-per-mile, but those behind him had slowed even more. Still, the race was far from over. Many experienced marathoners have led by wide margins with three-fourths of their run completed, only to fade badly and lose—and sometimes not even finish.

At the Boston Marathon in 1963, Olympic champion Abebe Bikila and Mamo Wolde burst to an early lead. The two Ethiopians set course records all the way through 20 miles. Then both faded badly, Bikila finishing fifth, Wolde staggering home in 12th place. The same could happen to Frank Shorter.

But at least one of the runners close behind Frank thought it would not. Kenny Moore, who had tied with Frank in the American Olympic trials, had given up hope. Kenny wrote later in *Sports Illustrated:*

"With nine miles to go we plunged into the greenery of the English Garden. People shouted that Shorter was one minute ahead. Wolde and I looked behind us. Clayton was gone. There was only a pale little man in white (Lismont), 150 yards back. The day had cooled. The next five miles through the park would be in shade. And Frank had said, 'I've never really died after getting a lead.' I believed him now. He could hold his minute. Wolde and I were running for silver."

In *The Frank Shorter Story* Frank discussed this moment in the race: "I don't really remember anything until I got into the English Garden, which is the far, long stretch where everyone was worried about the gravel. I never even thought about it. All I was really concentrating on in the English Garden was cutting corners, because the path really weaves. There was a lot of tangent running, trying to cut as straight a line as possible, considering that the side of the path was sloped, so you couldn't really take advantage of the whole path. I think this was one of the reasons that the time was a little slow. That must have made the course slower by two minutes.

"Once I got to the top of the English Garden, at

33

about 32 or 35 kilometers, I thought I had a good chance to win. By then I figured if I could make it to 40, it would be all over."

By 35 kilometers in 1:48:40 (15:51), Frank had stretched his lead now to 1:24 over Wolde. Moore suffered a cramp in his right hamstring muscle and saw his chance for a silver medal fade as Wolde moved away from him. Then Karel Lismont passed and Moore lost the bronze medal too. Only the first three finishers win awards in the Olympic Games. Kenny Moore now was running for pride.

Frank Shorter, meanwhile, was flying—buoyed by the cheers and applause of people jamming both sides of the road. The course at this point was slightly uphill. This did not worry Frank. Instead, it increased his confidence. He knew that if anyone expected to catch him on this stretch, they must run very hard to do so.

By 40 kilometers in 2:05:31 (15:51), he had extended his lead to 2:05 over Lismont, who had moved past Wolde. By now Frank knew that nothing could prevent his victory. He permitted himself a brief moment of exultation. "My God, I've really done it," he thought with less than a mile to go and the Olympic stadium in sight. The crowd in that stadium stilled, having been told by the track announcer that the leader in the marathon approached. A figure clad in running shorts and vest strode through the marathon gate and out onto the track for the final lap. The crowd screamed its approval.

But the runner was not Frank Shorter! It was someone else. Nor was it Lismont, Wolde, or Moore. The runner was an impostor, a non-runner who had darted onto the course ahead of Frank in the last mile of the race to claim the cheers earned by the winner.

The cheers quickly turned to boos as the crowd realized it was an impostor. And at that moment Frank

34

ran through the marathon gate and onto the track, puzzled, thinking for a moment that the boos were for him, wondering why there was another runner on the track ahead of him, worrying that maybe somebody had gotten ahead without his knowing it, then realizing this must be impossible.

He maintained the same steady pace he had held for the last half of the race. He made no attempt to sprint even though he was close to the record of 2:12:11.2 set by Bikila in 1964. "The last half mile is not the race," claims Frank Shorter. "It doesn't mean anything to sprint there. The real race is out between 15 and 40 kilometers."

His winning time was 2:12:19.8. He stopped, waved to the crowd, then walked back toward the finish line to greet the other runners as they came across: Lismont in 2:14:31.8; Wolde in 2:15:08.4; Moore, by now cramped in both legs, in 2:15:39.8; Japan's Kenji Kimihara in 2:16:27.0; Britain's Ron Hill in 2:16:30.6. The third American, Jack Bacheler, placed ninth in 2:17:38.2, with Australia's Derek Clayton, the world record holder, 13th in 2:19:49.7.

Frank Shorter walked a lap on the grass around the track as people shouted for his autograph and photographers yelled for him to pose for one more picture. It was then beginning to sink into him that he had won the gold medal in the Olympic marathon and his life would never quite be the same.

Yet he was still a runner. The day after his Olympic marathon victory he got up and ran five miles. The day after that he went twenty. He is still running today.

4
COMEBACK

Bill Rodgers watched Frank Shorter win the Olympic marathon in 1972 from a distance of about 5,000 miles. Bill was sitting in the apartment of his girl friend Ellen watching the Olympic Games on television. When he saw Frank cross the finish line, the first American Olympic marathon champion in sixty-four years, Bill had no idea that someday he might have a chance to do the same.

Bill Rodgers, then twenty-four, was only a year younger than Frank Shorter. He was born December 23, 1947 and grew up in Newington, a small town outside Hartford, Connecticut. His father was a professor, head of the Hartford State College Mechanical Engineering Department. His mother served as a nurse's aid at Newington Hospital, where Bill worked summers while in high school. At the time of the 1972 Olympics, Bill had a job as an orderly at Peter Bent Bingham Hospital in Boston.

Like many long distance runners, Bill Rodgers is slender: 5 feet 8½ inches, 128 pounds. He has long blond hair, granite-like features, and his typical expression is quizzical. When someone offers him some information, he often will not respond immediately, but rather say,

"Mmmmm," as though he wants to consider what he has heard before replying. Then his reply may be short and studied, like "Bizarre"—or, if someone has told him about a rival who is running well: "Impending doom!"

Yet there is a cheerful attitude about this intense man. Amby Burfoot, his roommate from college, describes him by saying, "Rodgers hasn't changed at all since his college days. He's still like a little puppy wagging his tail, hoping to please and waiting to play."

Bill had run with some success in high school and college, but unlike Frank Shorter who had dedicated himself to becoming an Olympic athlete after graduating from Yale, Bill stopped running even before his graduation from Wesleyan. He started smoking cigarettes. He hung around bars drinking beer. Only after several years did he begin running again, during the winter of 1972.

"I had experienced a certain level of fitness and I knew what it was like," he told a reporter from the publication *New England Running*. "I can remember waking up one morning early in 1972 with this noise in my chest, wheezing. It felt terrible. That, combined with some other things, got me running again."

Bill Rodgers always had been active as a boy growing up in Newington. He had one brother, Charlie, who was a year older, and two younger sisters. Charlie and Bill often did things together: ten-mile hikes in the woods, exploring, and camping out. "We'd sometimes get up around 3:00 A.M. and walk five miles to go fishing in a lake," recalls Bill. "I used to play touch football and baseball and I really liked gym. I loved volleyball and even doing push-ups, chin-ups, sit-ups and all that."

The father of one of his friends had been a runner back in the 1930s. One day he told Bill: "You're going to be a good runner some day." This was before Bill even thought he might try the sport.

His first early races were on field days in grade school. He usually ran well. In gym class in junior high he ran a distance of about a half mile long and had the second fastest time. In tenth grade at Newington high school he competed in an intramural cross-country program and took first place.

His first coach in tenth grade knew little about training track runners, and the team captain was a weight lifter. Training consisted mostly of calisthenics: push-ups, jumping jacks, touching toes. Bill thrived on this, however, enjoying the excitement of competing against the other people on his team, seeing how well he could do. They ran laps in the school hall to get their legs in shape. The first time Bill ran in a track meet, he did 5:20 for the mile. He competed in only three races that spring, but won two of them.

The following year, Frank O'Rourke, a former half miler at Boston University, became the track coach at Newington High School. O'Rourke trained the team by what is known as the "interval" method: a fast 220, 440, or 880, followed by a short interval of jogging. Sometimes the team ran on the track; other times they ran on roads, sprinting one way then jogging back.

During Bill's senior year in high school he won the Connecticut Class A (for smaller schools) cross-country race and placed seventh in the New England Championships. In track he ran 4:28.8 for the mile and 9:36 for the two mile, good times but not great ones. Frank Shorter, who graduated from high school one year before Bill, had run about the same.

At one point, Bill's parents asked his coach about Bill's potential as a runner. Did he have a chance to become a champion in college? "I wouldn't get your hopes too high," suggested Coach O'Rourke. Bill's parents advised Bill to quit running and concentrate on his studies.

38

Nevertheless, several colleges saw enough promise in Bill Rodgers to offer him athletic scholarships. One was Wesleyan University, a school of about 1600 students in Middletown, Connecticut. Bill enrolled in Wesleyan in the fall of 1965. The number-one runner at Wesleyan at this time was Amby Burfoot, who a few years later (in 1968) would be the first American in eleven years to win the Boston Marathon. Foreign runners from Finland, Japan or Belgium usually won that prestigious event. The last previous American winner (1957) had been John J. Kelley, who had coached Amby in high school.

Bill began running regularly with Amby and the other runners on the Wesleyan team. Amby and Bill roomed together Bill's sophomore year. Unlike the fast interval training Bill did in high school, most of their workouts were long, steady, comfortable distance runs. Their aim was developing a base of conditioning. On weekends they often would go for a 15-mile run. For a full week, Bill would average 50 to 70 miles.

Improvement came slowly, however. His time as a freshman of 9:23 for two miles was only slightly better than his high school best. As a sophomore he ran 4:18 for the mile and 9:23 in the two-mile. Then Amby graduated, and without his former roommate and training partner, Bill Rodgers lost some of his motivation. He failed to improve as a junior in 1968.

But that spring Amby won the Boston Marathon, and Bill Rodgers caught a glimpse of what he too might achieve. The following summer he worked harder than he had any previous vacation, running five miles in the morning, then five miles in the afternoon. "I had the idea that this was going to be the end of my track career," he says. "It often is for most people in college." He ran a ten-mile road race in Meriden, Connecticut, placing second. He placed 13th in the New England cross-country championships that fall. During the indoor track season that winter, he ran 8:58 for two miles, well below his previous best. Then he quit running. "I wanted to apply myself to some school work which had really piled up," he says. That two-mile was the last race he ran for nearly three years.

After graduation, Bill worked in the post office as a substitute letter carrier. In the spring of 1971, he got a job in Boston working as an orderly at Peter Bent Brigham Hospital as an alternate form of service to going into the Army. Once or twice a week he would run, usually five miles. Soon he stopped doing even this. He was still interested in running as a sport, and he watched track meets on TV. On Patriot's Day, Bill stood with the crowd watching the thousands who ran each year in the Boston Marathon.

He started smoking cigarettes, not so much because he liked it, but because others around him smoked. His job was grim: washing dishes, emptying bedpans, taking bodies down to the morgue.

Bad luck plagued him. He had two ten-speed bicycles stolen from him. Then thieves stole his Triumph 650 motorcycle. "That was my pride and joy," says Bill Rodgers, still sad over its loss.

The thefts meant Bill no longer had transportation from his apartment to the hospital, a mile and a half away. "I hate the subway and I can't stand walking in the city," Bill claims, "so I decided to run to and from work."

Once back running, he realized that he still enjoyed the sport. He cut down on his smoking, then quit entirely. He joined the Huntington Avenue YMCA around the corner from where he lived, running during the winter on the Y's 12½-lap-to-the-mile indoor track. He ran at the Y three or four times a week, building himself up to running

40

ten miles on Saturdays. "That was something," he says, "125 laps on that rinky-dinky track."

At the hospital, he became involved in trying to organize a union among the hospital orderlies and got fired. Temporarily out of a job, Bill had more time on his hands, so he began to increase the level of his running.

By then he lived near Jamaica Pond, a popular training area among Boston runners. Bill would run five miles around the pond in the morning and return in the afternoon to go ten. His longest run was 20 miles. It was steady-paced running, with no speed work. Soon he was averaging 100 miles a week, more than he ever had while on the track team at Wesleyan.

In February, 1973, Bill Rodgers ran his first race in three years and placed third, covering 20 miles in 1:44. The following month he placed second in another 30-kilometer race, then won a 12-miler. He entered the Boston Marathon in April, hoping to finish with a time somewhere in the mid-2:20s, a reasonable goal considering his other results.

"It was a very warm day," recalls Bill. "I had a stitch in my side during the first mile, my breathing seemed off, and after seven miles I was on the side of the road. I started running again, but hordes of people passed me going up the Newton hills. I eventually made it, stop and go, as far as 21 miles, but it was a futile effort."

After his failure to finish Boston, Bill quit running for two months. Unhappy with his performance in hot weather, he thought maybe he needed to train in the heat. He drove to California to see what living in that state might be like, but after a few days went back to Boston.

Bill began training again, running twice a day, an hour each workout. He got a job teaching retarded children at the Walter E. Fernald School. Since he had charge

41

of his own ward, he could juggle his work hours to allow himself time to train during the day. He would run an hour and a half in the morning, then work from 3:00 to 11:00, and run another hour during his supper break. He often trained on hills to increase his strength.

That fall, he won the National AAU 20-kilometer championship. He also finished his first 26-mile race, the Bay State Marathon in Framingham, Massachusetts. Bill began that race slowly, running the first 16 miles easily to make certain he would finish, and then moving in after the leaders. He caught them two miles from the finish and won in 2:28:12.

He began training under Billy Squires, coach of the Greater Boston Track Club. Squires' runners trained on the Boston College track, doing interval workouts several days a week at distances from 440 yards to one-and-a-half miles. This added speed work complemented the basic long-distance running Bill had been doing for the past two years.

In April 1974, Bill entered his second Boston Marathon. At the start he followed the fast early pace of Neil Cusack of Ireland (the eventual winner), Tom Fleming, and Lucien Rosa. But midway through the race, his legs began to cramp. Going through the Newton hills between 18 and 22 miles, runners began to pass him again. He moved off to the side of the road to massage his legs.

At that moment John Vitale, one of the runners he sometimes trained with, went by. Vitale shouted, "Get back in here!"

Bill looked up, uncertain whether or not to quit. At that stage in the race Vitale seemed as though he was hardly moving. "He was moving like a tortoise," recalls Bill. "I thought, 'If he can go that slow, I can run that slow.'" Bill started running again. He had to stop and

42

walk several times more, but he still finished in 14th place with a time of 2:19:34.

It was Bill Rodgers' first finish at Boston, and a good finish, but it would not be his best finish in that classic of world long-distance running events.

5
HOPKINTON

Other than the Olympic marathon itself, the most important 26-mile 385-yard race in the world is the Boston Marathon, run each April on Patriot's Day. That holiday is on the third Monday in April, celebrated in New England. It honors Paul Revere's ride on April 19, 1775, to warn people of the approach of British troops during the American Revolution.

Since most people are off work and the race is free to spectators, it has become a popular pastime in Boston to watch the marathon. In fact, the Boston Marathon has become the best attended sporting event in the world. Twenty-six miles of people, four and five deep, jam the course from its start in suburban Hopkinton to the downtown Prudential Center. In some crowded areas, such as Wellesley near the halfway point, people spill out onto the road, narrowing the course to two or three runners wide.

In addition to being the most watched sporting event in the world, the Boston Marathon is the oldest continually held marathon. Only the Olympic marathon, which began in 1896, is older. Boston dates back to 1897 and has been held in the same city every year since.

The fact that Boston started its marathon one year after the Olympics is no coincidence. A group of athletes and officials from the Boston Athletic Association attended the first Olympic Games in Greece in 1896. Impressed by the long-distance race from Marathon to Athens, the B.A.A. decided to start a similar "marathon" in Boston the following spring.

Even though a million people might turn out on a sunny April day to watch the Boston Marathon, those who ran it numbered only a few hundred until the mid 1960s. Few people ran marathons until that time. Those who did were usually fast, dedicated athletes, many of them with Olympic ambitions.

But in 1962 *Sports Illustrated* published an article about the Boston Marathon and the people who ran it. This focused attention on the event. In 1968 Kenneth H. Cooper, M.D., wrote *Aerobics,* a book that promoted jogging as a means to better health. More and more people started to run as one way to prevent heart attacks. Some of those people set as their goals running in the Boston Marathon, even though they had no chance to win it.

Then, when Frank Shorter won the marathon in the Olympics in 1972, he was catapulted into the position of great fame. Frank became a national sports hero like Pete Rose in baseball, Roger Staubach in football, or Mario Andretti in auto racing.

Few people can compete in the World Series with Rose, in the Super Bowl with Staubach, or in the Indy 500 with Andretti. But almost anyone can run a marathon with Shorter. Unlike most major sports, all you need to do to participate in a marathon is train for it. With the exception of the Olympics, and lately Boston, most marathons in the world are open to anybody who wants to enter. Running them has become a popular participant sport.

As a result, the fields in the Boston Marathon have doubled in size, then doubled again. Instead of a few hundred running from Hopkinton to Prudential each Patriot's Day, there were suddenly a few thousand. The crowds of people watching the race also increased.

In 1970, the Boston Athletic Association imposed a time standard to attempt to limit the field to a manageable 1,000 or so runners. They required that all entrants have run a marathon in 3:30. A few years later, they lowered that standard further to 3:00 for male runners under the age of forty. Women and men over forty could still qualify with 3:30.

Rather than limiting the field, however, the time standard seemed to *attract* more runners. Anyone bettering the Boston "standard" in another race would be told by his friends: "Well, you qualified for Boston." Thus that person would feel obligated to enter the Boston Marathon the next year. Many runners trained specially for Boston. They made it their goal. There was status for those good enough to run at Boston.

Many of those who failed to meet the qualifying standard ran Boston anyway. Refused an official number, they started in the back of the pack. By 1975 the number of official starters at Boston numbered 2100 with hundreds more starting without numbers.

In that same year Bill Rodgers seemed ready to emerge as one of the top long-distance runners in the United States. Few had heard of Bill, but people in New England began to recognize his ability.

During the winter of 1975, Bill traveled south to Gainesville, Florida, to compete in the American trials for the international cross-country championships. Although he had been sick several days earlier in the week, he placed fourth. This placing earned him a position on the seven-man American team that would compete against squads from Europe and other parts of the world in a race held in Morocco in North Africa in March.

The Morocco race was held on a flat 12-kilometer course of several laps that started and finished at a horse race track. The runners hurdled several barriers each lap and ran through a ditch. Bill started slowly, falling behind the leaders by as much as 100 yards, but by two miles he moved up to the front along with Ian Stewart of Great Britain and Mariano Haro of Spain.

The three ran together most of the way. Several times, Bill attempted to surge away from Stewart and Haro, but they stayed with him. With a half mile to go, coming through a ditch, Stewart and Haro sprinted. Bill faded, but still placed third, just ahead of New Zealand's John Walker, who later set the world record in the 1,500 meters and won the Olympic gold medal in that event.

Bill was thrilled by his good finish in such a tough international race. He did not even feel tired. He ran back to his hotel, a mile and a half, and later that day went for a seven-mile run. But he tried to downplay his ability. Later he told his former roommate Amby Burfoot: "It was a fluke. I don't belong with those guys. It was the race of my life. I'll probably never run that well again."

Entering the 1975 Boston Marathon, Bill Rodgers hoped only to run up to his ability—and perhaps improve slightly on his 2:19 time from the previous year.

"I don't want to go out too fast this year," he said to Burfoot the day before the race. "I did that last year and paid the price. I'd like to tuck in behind Hill, Dryton, Fleming, Mabuza, and Vitale. I figure they'll be the leaders, and I'll just try to stick with them. If I have a good day, I may be able to hit 2:16 or something around there."

The night before the race Bill had macaroni and cheese for dinner. He slept well, awoke early, and had pancakes for his final training meal. At about 10:00 A.M. he drove to suburban Hopkinton, where the race started at noon.

Hopkinton is a small town of 4100 people, conveniently located 26 miles from downtown Boston. With the exception of the first year, 1897, the Boston Marathon always has begun in Hopkinton, although the exact starting line has been moved slightly within the town several times.

Mid-April is usually a pleasant time of year in Boston. The trees are about to bloom. The weather varies, depending on shifts of the winds. It can be cold, almost freezing, or very warm. But it is a good time of year to run marathons.

The countryside crossed by the Boston Marathon is hilly and rolling, with the start several hundred feet higher in elevation than the finish. Near the starting line, you can look toward Boston and see the mammoth Prudential Tower, where the race finishes, sticking up on the horizon like a tiny needle. It is a frightening sight for the runners, who must cover 26 miles on foot to get there.

The runners dress at the Hopkinton high school gym. They sit in the bleachers or spread out over the basketball floor, blanketing almost every square foot of empty space. A few of the fast runners gather in a side dressing room where members of the press interview them before the race.

Runners also spill out into the parking lot beside the school or onto the athletic fields behind it. They warm up by jogging on the grass or sit and stretch to relax their muscles. They talk to friends or stand in lines to go to the toilets. Outside the school grounds salesmen hawk all sorts of goods, from T-shirts saying "Boston Marathon" to postcards and maps of New England.

When he arrived just before 11 A.M., Bill Rodgers moved quietly through the mob, unrecognized by any except a few of the New England runners who knew him. He picked up his number 14, signifying his place the previous year. He pinned it to his T-shirt, on which he had

48

hand-lettered the name BOSTON and below that the letters GBTC, which stood for the Greater Boston Track Club.

Many of the top marathoners are sought after by shoe companies: Adidas, Nike, Tiger, Puma, Brooks. Running shoes are the most important item worn by any runner. Good running shoes cost $30 or more. A shoe recognized as being fast or comfortable will earn millions of dollars for its manufacturer. Some shoe companies give fast runners free shoes and even pay them to wear their models.

No company had as yet shown much interest in Bill Rodgers. He laced on a pair of Nike shoes, which he had purchased himself, then put on a headband advertising New Balance, another brand of running shoe. Then he donned an ordinary green sweat suit and went to the starting line.

The starting line in Hopkinton is located nearly a mile from the gym. Years ago, runners climbed on buses to ride this distance, not wishing to cover any more mileage than necessary on race day. But the crowds pressing around the gym and on the road between the gym and the starting line are so great now that most runners walk or jog the distance. Soon after 11:30 A.M. Bill Rodgers joined this slowly moving crowd of runners headed for the line.

Recently those in charge of the Boston Marathon have organized the runners before the start according to time. Those expected to average 6:00-per-mile stand in a block ahead of 7:00-runners, who stand before 8:00-runners. They are separated by ropes.

The fast runners, those with low numbers on their shirts like Bill Rodgers, have reserved starting positions in the front. They stand directly behind the white line painted across the street. Officials, reporters, and photographers swarm around them like bees.

Five minutes before noon, Bill Rodgers shed his

49

sweat suit and handed it to a friend who went with him to the line. He took his position among those near the front. He jogged nervously in place, shaking his hands to remain relaxed. It was a cool day and he wore white cotton gloves on his hands.

Marathoners like the weather cool, because it allows them to run faster times. When TV weather forecasters in Boston say on Sunday night that the weather on Monday will be sunny and warm and nice for the marathon, they mean nice for *watching* the marathon, not running it. Ideal running weather is around 50 degrees, maybe even with a light drizzle, but no wind unless it is at the runners' backs. Since Boston is a point-to-point race, winds from the west sometimes help push runners to fast times.

In the last few minutes before the start, people began to grow silent. Runners crossed themselves, or bent to tie shoelaces, or just stared straight ahead. They grasped hands and wished each other luck. They adjusted wristwatches to keep track of their times.

Officials gave the fidgeting runners reports on the time remaining: "Two minutes to go." Then: "One minute to go." The reporters and photographers moved out of the way. Police pushed people back onto the curbs.

Finally, the gun sounded.

6
DAY OF GLORY

A roar erupted from the thousands of spectators crowded into Hopkinton Square as the runners in the front row sprinted across the line. And at the same time a cheer rose from the many of the runners themselves, particularly those back in the pack. Many raised fists in the air and shook them, as though to celebrate a victory. For most of the runners at Boston, *being* in this great race was a victory.

Those in the middle of the pack cheered not only themselves and those around them, but also the fast runners who quickly disappeared from their view. Most of the pack would not see those runners again and would only hear of them as they caught snatches of information from radios held by spectators along the route. When the first runners crossed the finish line at Boston, others would be miles behind, some with an hour or two of running remaining.

Bill Rodgers was one of those fast runners who moved quickly at the sound of the gun, partly to stay with the leaders and partly out of fear. He did not want to get trampled by those behind. He did not want them getting in his way, slowing him down. Yet he was afraid of going too fast and fading, the way he had in his two previous

51

Boston starts. He allowed the front runners to move away from him, but carefully kept them in sight.

They were moving down a slight incline following Route 135, the highway linking Hopkinton with Boston. The start at Boston is always fast, partly because it is downhill. Hopkinton is roughly 500 feet above the near-sea-level finish in downtown Boston. More than 300 feet of that drop occurs in the first half dozen miles. But the start is also fast because all the runners are keyed up. They have been training for and looking forward to this moment for a year. There is also the cheering of the crowd, which inspires the runners to push to the limits of their ability and sometimes beyond.

As always, a few slow runners sneaked up near the front and sprinted hard, hoping to get their pictures in the paper the next day leading the Boston Marathon, if only at the start. But they paid for the foolishness. Within a few hundred yards, they had already begun to drop back.

Other, faster runners also sprinted beyond their ability, hoping that this might be the day when they could make a vast improvement in their previous marathon best, maybe even win the race. "You can never tell when you'll run a blazer," said Bernie Allen of England, who soon took the lead. The fast runners who misjudged their pace also would pay for their errors—although it might not be for 15 or 20 miles. Then they would drop back, spent, grimacing, clutching their sides, some unable to finish.

The marathon is a race with many winners and few losers. The ones who drop out are the only losers.

Bill Rodgers did not want to be one of the losers, so he waited. He ran comfortably off the pace. He allowed the early sprinters to get 50 then 100 yards ahead of him. He ran without panic. When the time was right, he would gently reel them back in.

Bill did not wait long. He judged that the front

runners were running a comfortable, not frantic, pace. After a mile and a half, he moved up and caught the front group of about a dozen runners, including Allen.

He made no attempt to pass, but stayed within the group, allowing the momentum of their joint effort to carry him along.

There was no traffic on the four-lane highway. Other than vehicles for officials and press, and one flatbed truck with bleacher seats in back that carried photographers, no automobiles were permitted on the road with the runners.

The runners shifted from one side to the other as the highway wound its way toward Boston. When the highway veered left, they moved to its left side. They cut the turn at its apex as a driver would in an automobile race. Then as the highway turned right, they moved across the center stripe and toward the right shoulder.

They hoped to trace the straightest possible line toward the finish. Even in a race of 25,000 steps, they did not want to waste a single step, a single foot, a single tick of the watch in their movement toward downtown Boston. They might need everything they gained 26 miles farther down the road when they had to outkick another runner or beat a specific time.

The specter of Dorando Pietri haunted them. Perhaps that Italian who collapsed within sight of the finish line at the 1908 Olympics had wasted some yardage that could have brought him, unaided, across the line for a gold medal.

Even in the gently downward-rolling hills between Hopkinton and the next town of Framingham, people lined the sides of the road. They stood in front of their houses. They sat atop parked cars. Little boys and girls waited by the side of the road, offering orange slices to the passing runners.

Orange slices are among the traditions of the Boston Marathon. Few among the leaders would take orange slices in this early stage of the race, but someone far back in the pack of runners would accept the slices, grateful for the thought behind them. The boys and girls would be happy that, even in their own small way, they had been part of the 1975 Boston Marathon. Maybe one day they might be running it themselves.

As the runners entered the town of Framingham and approached the first checkpoint at 6.7 miles, the crowds by the side of the road increased. Framingham is the site of a famous health study undertaken in the 1940s. The Framingham Study sought to prove that physical exercise is good for your health. Doctors who believe that running can help prevent heart attacks mention Framingham as part of their evidence. However, though many in the two thousand participating in the Boston Marathon that day may have begun running to improve their health, few worried about health or fitness at that moment. They were part of a great race, and they ran for the challenge and enjoyment—not health.

Near the actual checkpoint across from the railroad station in downtown Framingham, the crowds spilled out onto the street, forcing the runners into a increasingly narrow path. A triangular orange sign set in the middle of the road announced: 19½ MILES TO GO. One of the oddities of the Boston Marathon is that its checkpoints come at irregular intervals. In most other races runners receive times at even points, such as five kilometers, or five miles. Not at Boston. Boston is steeped in traditions difficult to break.

As Bill Rodgers swept past the orange triangle at the Framingham checkpoint, he remained caught in the center of the pack. Bill gave the time called to him little attention. If he had, he might have realized that he passed that classic point 29 seconds slower than Ron Hill in 1970 when Ron set the Boston Marathon record of 2:10:30. But time meant nothing to Bill, only victory.

Just beyond Framingham, however, Jerome Drayton of Canada and Mario Cuezas of Mexico began to push the pace. Bill allowed them to pull 20 yards ahead of him. He knew they were moving fast, maybe too fast, but he did not want to risk letting them leave him behind.

Bill also knew that Drayton had a reputation for running too hard at the start, then burning out. In 1970, when Ron Hill set his record, Jerome ran even with Ron, then quit. The Canadian often failed to finish, particularly when another runner followed his hard early pace and challenged him. But in other races when no one stayed with Drayton's burning pace to challenge him near the end, the Canadian often finished in record times.

Bill could not risk running too fast, but neither could he risk allowing Drayton or Cuezas to leave him. One of them might burn out, but one of them might go on to rob him of victory. Within a mile he caught the pair. So fast was the pace of the three leaders at this point that they reached the 10.4-mile checkpoint in the next town of Natick, only two seconds behind Hill's record pace.

Bill later admitted: "I kept thinking, 'I've done it again. Too fast. I'll crack just like last year.' My legs were tight at seven or eight miles and I knew we were running fast even though I hadn't heard any of the times."

Nevertheless, Bill Rodgers continued to push on toward the halfway point at Wellesley like a man gone mad. He reached the 13.4-mile checkpoint in Wellesley 10 yards in front, running 11 seconds under record pace. The temperature was perfect for running marathons: 50 degrees. The westerly wind, gusting at 15 to 25 mph, was at the backs of the runners. It was a good day to run fast.

The crowds in Wellesley pressed into the street, narrowing the corridor through which Bill ran to a thin

55

alley. Most of the spectators at this point were students at Wellesley College, a women's institution. There were 49 women running the Boston Marathon that day, in addition to 2,041 men, and the students waited to cheer those of their own sex. But until the first woman appeared back in the pack, they were happy to cheer the first man.

"The noise was incredible," said Bill. "It actually scared me, but was great at the same time because it kept me going."

The crowds recognized Bill Rodgers as one of them because he had hand-lettered *Boston* on the front of his shirt. It had not been since the victory of Johnny Kelley in 1957 that someone identified as a Bostonian had won the Boston Marathon.

The crowds cheered Rodgers even though at first they did not know his name. Those who brought newspapers with them to the course looked up his number. The Boston *Globe* carried the complete list of entries in its morning edition. They saw that number 14 belonged to Bill Rodgers and cheered him by name: "Come on, Bill! You can do it!"

Then as Bill moved into the lead and the distance between him and Jerome Drayton running in second increased to 50, then 100, then 200 yards, word spread along the route that Bill Rodgers of the Greater Boston Track Club was leading the Boston Marathon. The closer he got to the finish line the louder became the cheers for him.

But there was still a long way to go, and Bill was worried. "I don't know what made me go to the front," he said later. "Sometimes I think I have a suicidal instinct. But once I was there, I figured I'd better go hard to build a lead, so I pushed it down the hills out of Wellesley."

At the 17.6-mile checkpoint in Auburndale, Rodgers was 38 seconds ahead of Hill's record pace, but he suddenly slowed to a stop. He drank from a cup of water offered him. It was one of several water stops he made. "I know everyone thinks I'm crazy to stop," he said later, "but I think it helps me. If I don't stop, I can't drink—it just splashes. I only got down a couple of gulps each time, but I needed it."

By now he was into the Newton Hills. There are four hills within the town of Newton, roughly between 18 and 20 miles of the marathon route. They come one after another without letup. The final hill is called "Heartbreak Hill," perhaps the most famous hill on any marathon course. It is so named because the Boston Marathon often is won or lost on this hill as one runner pulls away from another. Many fine runners have met their downfall on Heartbreak Hill. And many slower runners as well.

Part of the reason for this is that Heartbreak Hill comes at a point, about three-quarters into the race, when the energy of the runners has drained away. The exuberance that carried them off the starting line at a too-fast pace is forgotten. They are tired, thirsty, possibly hot. Their muscles ache. Blisters have begun to bother their feet. Their clothing chafes them. Minor discomforts become major ones when stretched over a period of several hours.

Even in a one-mile race, the three-quarter point is the point of maximum stress. You have gone far enough and fast enough to be very tired, but you are not close enough and fast enough yet to start your final sprint to the finish. In a mile run, a miler who has overpaced himself reaching the three-quarter point has only one lap, a quarter mile, to stagger in to the finish. A marathoner who suffers a similar lapse of judgment has six long miles to run—and he may not finish.

After running seemingly without effort through the first three of the Newton hills, Bill Rodgers suddenly stopped at the foot of Heartbreak Hill. As his body warmed, Bill took off the white gloves he wore at the start of the race. He carried them in his hands, and now he bent, placed them on the street, and calmly tied his shoelaces. "The shoes were getting loose," he said, "so I thought I better retie them before the situation got serious. What better place than the foot of Heartbreak Hill? It relaxed me, gave me a mental break from the pace."

He probably lost only 15 or 20 seconds, but could he waste even that much time? Recalling that several runners had passed in the last few miles the previous year, he glanced back over his shoulder as he ran down Commonwealth Avenue, the wide, divided boulevard which the course follows most of the last four miles.

"About two miles from the finish line," Bill said, "I began to think I might win if my legs didn't cramp on me. I kept looking behind me for Drayton, but the crowd had narrowed to a small gap behind me." Bill worried that somehow Drayton might sneak up from the side and jump out of the crowd almost on top of him.

But Jerome Drayton would not threaten that day. Bill Rodgers' fast pace had broken him. As Jerome slowed, he was passed by Tom Fleming of New Jersey, who had placed second at Boston in 1973 and 1974. Drayton began to jog. Steve Hoag of the Twin Cities Track Club passed, dropping Jerome another position. He started to walk.

When England's Ron Hill came by a few minutes later, he saw Drayton sitting on the side of the road. "Get going!" Hill yelled at him. "Walk if you have to, but finish the race." Drayton failed to move.

Bill Rodgers had now almost reached downtown Boston. The crowds lining the course grew thicker and thicker. People leaned out windows of their apartments to see the race. Kids clung to trees and lampposts for a better view. The noise grew deafening as it became obvious that

58

someone from Boston would win the Boston Marathon. The sound of cheering rolled down Commonwealth Avenue in Bill Rodgers' wake.

Bill turned right onto Hereford Street and now he had only a half mile to run. A quarter mile farther, he turned left at Boylston Street and onto the ramp in front of Prudential Center and the Sheraton Hotel. He could see the finish line down a slight incline with less than 385 yards of the 26-mile 385-yard race to be covered.

Spectators had jammed into the several-block-long area around the finish line. They formed a bowl into which he now ran. Maybe as many as 50,000 people crowded into the area to see the winner of the Boston Marathon as he crossed the line. It was Bill Rodgers in 2:09:55, a new Boston record, an American record, and the fifth fastest time run in the world to that date.

The next person around the corner was Steve Hoag, who passed Fleming in the last few miles. They ran 2:11:54, and 2:12:05. It was the first time since 1942 that Americans finished one-two-three. Canada's Jerome Drayton failed to finish. Despite being thoroughly beaten, he would return to Boston two years later to win the race. But for the time being, it was Bill Rodgers' day of glory.

7
THE WOMEN OF BOSTON

At the moment Bill Rodgers crossed the finish line at Prudential Center and had the laurel wreath of victory thrust upon his head, Gayle Barron of Atlanta had barely crested Heartbreak Hill. Gayle learned that Bill had won because many people watching the race had portable radios tuned to the marathon broadcast. They shouted the news to the runners, who passed the information back and forth among each other.

Bill Rodgers had never heard of Gayle Barron at that time. But Gayle Barron had not heard of Bill Rodgers either. Gayle was new to competitive running. This was only her third marathon race.

Women were new to marathon running. They had been running the Boston Marathon less than ten years, since 1966 when Roberta Gibb Bingay of San Diego first ran the race unofficially.

Twenty-three years old, Roberta began running three years before because it was fun. Like many men, she focused on the Boston Marathon as one of her goals. For six months before Boston, she trained by running as much as 15 to 20 miles a day.

In 1966 there were no time-qualifying standards for Boston. Anybody supposedly could run. There was

60

not even an entry fee. The race was free to anyone who mailed in a blank. Two months before the 1966 race, Roberta mailed in her entry blank. It was returned with the comment: "Women are not allowed to enter."

This was in an era when the longest race for women in the Olympics, and most track meets, was 800 meters. Women ran cross-country races of only 1.5 miles long— and not too many of them did that. Women never entered road races at any distance, much less a marathon. The feeling among officials and coaches, both male and female, was that women were not strong enough to run long distances.

It was less a matter of rules prohibiting women from running long distances (although prohibitive rules did exist) than a lack of interest on the part of women to do so. Before 1966, few women showed a desire to run *any* distance. And few men too. In most parts of the country, 30 or 40 runners was considered a good field for a race at any distance. Some states did not have any races. The running explosion of the 1970s, where races with thousands of runners became almost common, had not yet occurred.

In 1966 Roberta Gibb Bingay decided to go to Boston to run the marathon despite her rejection by B.A.A. officials. She had married a sailor only three months before, but her husband was away on duty with a Navy sub-tender. Roberta rode a bus four days from San Diego to Boston. Dressed in a black bathing suit covered with light slacks cut at the knees, she hid in the bushes until the gun sounded. Then after about half the field had passed, she jumped out and joined the men.

Most men were surprised to see a woman running among them, but did not react at first. Boston is like a carnival at which anything can happen. People often jump out of the crowd to run along for a few hundred yards.

Sometimes they are wearing clown outfits or dressed as a gorilla, so why not a woman in a bathing suit? Most of the male runners regarded Roberta with silence.

Only after Roberta had run about five miles did it dawn on the male marathoners that she might be serious. "Hey, it's a girl!" runners began to say. "Fantastic! Good for you!" One asked her: "Hey, are you going all the way?"

"I hope so," Roberta replied, "if they don't throw me out."

When Roberta passed through Wellesley, the college students cheered wildly.

Roberta wrote later: "As the run progressed, an unexpected feeling of being valued and protected as a woman emerged. It's amazing. I was special not because I was running Boston, but because I was a woman."

She finished in the respectable time of 3:14, which put her somewhere in the middle of the field. The next morning the Boston *Record American* headlined her achievement: BRIDE BEATS 200 MEN IN MARATHON. Roberta returned to Boston to run unofficially again in 1967 and 1968. By then other women began to join her.

In 1967 Kathrine Switzer sent her entry in to Boston as "K. Switzer." She was accepted. Arriving in Hopkinton, Kathy sent her boyfriend into the gym to pass the physical examination then required of all runners and to pick up her number. Midway through the race, B.A.A. official Jock Semple spotted Kathy running with number attached and tried to rip it from her. Her boyfriend elbowed Jock out of the way and Kathy continued. Photographs of the incident made sports pages around the world.

Jock later insisted he did not object to Kathy's running in the race, only to her running with an "official number" gained illegally. (At one previous Boston Marathon, Jock had slugged someone who tried to join

62

the race wearing a gorilla costume.) Chided by the publicity given the incident, Jock Semple later became a major supporter of women in their efforts to gain acceptance in long-distance races.

More and more women began to appear at Boston and at other races where they were given numbers, despite A.A.U. rules forbidding it. Male runners began to encourage female runners. They recruited their wives and girl friends. Marathoning became a sport no longer restricted to "boys."

Finally in 1972 the B.A.A. surrendered and permitted women to enter Boston officially. They issued special numbers for female contestants and also offered trophies and medals for the first women across the line. Nina Kuscsik of New York won the women's section of the race that year with a time of 3:10:26.40.

By 1975 women were no longer considered freaks in marathons. Gayle Barron appeared in Boston that year without expecting to win or even place high among the women. She came hoping to break three hours for the first time, a goal considered worthy even for male runners. When the gun sounded, she started in the middle of the pack at a comfortable pace.

"I was probably running around 7:00 a mile, or slightly faster," Gayle recalled later. "I never carry a watch and I didn't hear any splits, but I was running relaxed. I noticed a lot of other girls go by me at the start, but this didn't concern me."

Joe Henderson of Pebble Beach, California, runner and author of many books, including *The Long Run Solution,* claims that there are two types of people who run marathons: Racers and Pacers. The Racers run mainly for position, the Pacers for time.

Joe explains: "Few runners can place well. The

competitors are too many and the prized positions too few. But anyone can go for a good time because the number available is unlimited.

"The Racers have to worry about other people—who enters, the kind of shape they're in, and the tactics they will use. The Pacers only have to be concerned with weather reports and pacing tables. It doesn't matter to them how they place, as long as the time is right."

Gayle Barron entered Boston that year as a Pacer, hopeful only of running a fast time. There were too many other runners around her, most of them men, for her to worry about beating them. And in the area of the country from where she came, the Deep South, there were very few female runners. During her short running career, she had run almost entirely with men.

But a strange thing happened on the way to Prudential Center. Without realizing it, Gayle changed from a Pacer to Racer. "It started when I came through Wellesley at the halfway point. There were so many girls shouting at me to do well that it really got my adrenalin pumping. I was running as fluidly as I ever had before. I started passing some of the people who passed me. Many of them were girls that I knew were good runners.

One of the runners Gayle passed was Joan Ullyot, M.D., author of the book *Women's Running*, and a sub three-hour runner. As Gayle passed, she heard Joan comment to her running companion: "Who is *she?*" Gayle smiled, but kept running.

At one point in the race, Gayle was passed by Nina Kuscsik, the 1972 winner. Nina, however, was on a bicycle. Injured, she had decided to cover the course by bike to encourage the woman runners. Nina did not know who Gayle was either, but she told her, "You're looking strong."

Liane Winter of West Germany won the women's
64

section of the Boston Marathon that day in 2:42:24, a new world record. Kathrine Switzer of New York finished second in 2:51:50. Crossing the finish line third in 2:54:29 was the newborn Racer from Atlanta, Gayle Barron.

Watching her cross the finish line was Ernst van Aaken, M.D., Winters' coach from Germany and a leading spokesman for women's marathoning. Dr. van Aaken could not speak English, but he asked Joan Ullyot to congratulate Gayle and tell her how strong she looked.

Dr. van Aaken later wrote of the race: "Gayle Barron of Atlanta (was) unknown to all the northerners. She'll have to be watched in the future, and perhaps is the runner with the most promise."

8
THE BARRONS OF PEACHTREE STREET

The surprising thing was not that Gayle Barron ran so well that day at Boston, but that she was running at all. When Gayle grew up in Decatur, a suburb of Atlanta, Georgia, girls did not run marathons.

Gayle was born on April 6, 1945, in Atlanta. Her father, Thomas Franklin Stocks, worked in a furniture store, but suffered from multiple sclerosis, which caused him to spend the last dozen years of his life bedridden. Her mother, Gloria, encouraged Gayle to take ballet lessons. Her older brother, Tom, showed more interest in business than sports. He eventually went into computer sales.

Nevertheless, Gayle enjoyed physical activity, or, as she admits, "I was sort of a tomboy. Most of my friends in the neighborhood were boys. I was interested in climbing trees. I loved to run. At night we'd go out and play kick the can."

She attended Druid Hills High School. The school offered only basketball and swimming for girls, and neither sport interested Gayle. She did enjoy physical education classes and might have become a physical education major at the University of Georgia except for peer pressure. So Gayle majored in public relations and adver-

66

tising and became a cheerleader. Each fall and spring she got into shape while cheerleading; the rest of the year she did little physically.

Then, while attending summer school in 1966 before the start of her senior year, she met Ben Barron. Ben was working toward a graduate degree in business. One of Gayle's girl friends arranged a blind date. Later, Ben asked Gayle to play tennis. She accepted, although she never had held a racket before. "It was a total disaster," Gayle recalls.

Ben astounded her because he always seemed to be in shape. When they met, Ben ran daily, sprinting up the stadium stairs, lifting weights. He was not training for any team. He exercised mainly for fun. This astounded Gayle. "Nobody works that hard for *fun*," she said.

Ben Barron stood 5 feet 11 inches and weighed 185 pounds. He had played basketball in high school, as well as football and baseball. He tried cross-country once in eighth grade, but did not care for it. Ben was the typical, medium-good athlete who, because of limits imposed by his size and ability, could not compete at a major university. Nevertheless, he kept physically fit.

Ben says of Gayle, "At that time there were not many athletic outlets for girls. When I met Gayle, I could see she was somebody with a certain amount of ability and interest, but she never had a chance to express herself."

Soon Ben and Gayle started having stadium dates. He ran a mile nonstop, which impressed her greatly. She ran maybe a quarter lap—all she could manage—then walked and jogged until he finished his mile. They walked together for a while, then she sat down while he ran up and down stadium steps.

The Georgia stadium contained 60 rows, 120 steps. Ben often ran up and down them 10 or 15 times, both front and backwards. Soon Gayle also began running stadium steps. She found that she enjoyed that as much as running in circles.

"If it were today, I probably would have pushed myself harder," she recalls, "but the fact that I was even out there doing something shocked me. The fact that I soon went a mile without even stopping was great. That was like, *'Look, I ran a mile!'* I told my mother and she thought I was nuts. All of my relatives thought I was crazy, so I decided not to talk about it anymore. I got very secretive about my running. I worried, maybe I shouldn't be doing this—but it made me feel so good."

If Gayle needed any endorsement, it came when she reported for cheerleading practice that fall. "The other girls couldn't believe how much weight I lost. I had always been rather large in the legs and thighs."

Ben graduated in December and moved from Athens back to Atlanta. Gayle did not enjoy running alone, so she quit. "I felt like an idiot by myself." When she went home on weekends, she ran with Ben at Northside High School. Later, after her graduation and return to Atlanta, they resumed a more regular running schedule. He worked as a stockbroker. Gayle got a job with an advertising agency, then a television station.

In the summer of 1969, Gayle and Ben Barron married. Running remained a regular part of their life. On Saturdays they would take a radio to Northside track and listen to the Georgia football game. "We would be at the track two or three hours and never see one person," recalls Gayle. "Now you can hardly find an empty lane, there are so many joggers."

Gayle's running leveled off around two miles a day, but she became more secure about it. "I didn't care if people laughed at me anymore," she says. "I'd run sometimes with Ben and sometimes alone. But always on the track. We never thought of running on the streets."

68

Ben worked downtown and joined the YMCA to run on its 26-lap-per-mile indoor track. One day he looked at the bulletin board and noticed an entry blank for a six-mile run on the Fourth of July: the Peachtree Race. It was 1971, the first year the Atlanta Track Club sponsored that event. By that time, the Barrons had increased their training to three miles. Ben thought it might be interesting to see if they could go six.

"I mentioned it to Gayle," smiles Ben. "She thought that running a race was the most stupid thing she had ever heard. But she wasn't about to let me go off and run it alone and come home bragging about it."

Two other women entered the race, probably feeling as foolish as Gayle Barron did about standing there among all those men. And there were not that many men either; only 110. The winner was Jeff Galloway, who had attended Wesleyan University at the same time as Bill Rodgers and later trained with Frank Shorter on the Florida Track Club.

The Barrons ran together at a comfortable 8:00-per mile pace, finishing in 49:15. This earned Gayle a first place. The officials awarded Gayle a trophy topped by the figure of a male runner. "I still have that trophy," says Gayle. "That's one I cherish more than any of them."

So Peachtree became the Barrons' Annual Race, Gayle finishing first woman the next four years, a fact that impresses others more than her. "Everybody says, 'Wow, you won the race four years in a row.' Yeah, but there never were more than five girls the whole time. Now there are hundreds." (The Peachtree Race in 1979 had 20,000 competitors, male and female.)

Following their first race, the Barrons' confidence in their running ability grew. They began to increase their mileage to four to six miles.

By then, running around a track had become bor-

69

ing to them. Ben sometimes worked late, so Gayle would run streets near their apartment in Buckhead, a northern suburb of Atlanta. "Dogs were my biggest problem," she remembers. "Then truck drivers. They always have to blow the horn at you, but they do that even if you are only walking." To fend off dogs Gayle carried a stick, and later a spray gun. Truck drivers, she learned to ignore.

Then in December 1972 Ben announced at the breakfast table, "There's a marathon today. I think I'll go run it."

"You're kidding," Gayle scoffed.

"No, I've always wondered how far I could go in a marathon."

"You're crazy," said Gayle, aware that neither of them ever had run past eight miles.

"No, I'm going to do it."

Gayle tried to change Ben's mind, without success. Just before he walked out the door, she said, "Wait a minute. I'm going with you."

The race was the Peach Bowl Marathon, run over a hilly two-lap course. They started slowly. Gayle recalls, "The first loop we felt good. I mean, not great, but we felt better than terrible. We thought we would see how much farther we could make—maybe even go the whole way. We kept talking, encouraging each other.

"We got to 16 miles, where we encountered this impossible hill. It's where most of the dropouts occur on the course. I never had a feeling like that before. It was really the wall. My legs ached from head to toe. My body ached and if I walked I felt worse. When I tried to run again, I almost fell to the ground.

"I told Ben, '*I just can't go any further.*' I looked around and I couldn't see anybody. Nobody else was on the course. It was so discouraging. By four in the afternoon it was getting dark. We didn't drink any fluids. We thought that would make us sick."

But the Barrons went on, finishing the race around 4:12. "One official with a bored look on his face, holding a stopwatch, waited to greet us," recalls Ben. "He had heard somebody was still running. Everybody else was in the gym getting awards."

It took Gayle Barron two weeks to recover from the ordeal. So sore she could barely walk, she sat in the tub for hours, trying to regain use of her body. She swore off marathons and in 1973 stood on the sidelines while Ben ran a solo 3:38. (His personal record, achieved in 1977 at the Fiesta Bowl Marathon, is 2:49.)

Nevertheless, whether or not Gayle recognized it, others thought she had talent, including Tim Singleton, an official with the Atlanta Track Club. He encouraged her to give the marathon one more try, feeling she had more endurance than speed. Singleton supervised her training two months before the 1974 Peach Bowl Marathon. She ran 50 miles a week, including a long run every weekend. Gayle began at 12 miles and eventually worked her way up to 18. By then she had been running eight years and had a good background of endurance.

She ran 3:06, qualifying to run the Boston Marathon. At Boston in 1975 Gayle ran 2:54:29, placing third. That fall at the New York City Marathon (then run around a four-lap course in Central Park) she placed third in 2:57:22, behind Kim Merritt and Miki Gorman. This qualified Gayle for the American team that would compete in the Women's International Marathon sponsored by Dr. Ernst van Aaken in Germany that following summer.

"Van Aaken treated us like queens," Gayle recalls of that race. "It was something different for me to spend

71

an entire week with other women runners. I had been running all my life with guys. I made a lot of friends and found that women are really neat as athletes.

"There was a sense of friendship, all of us getting nervous and pulling for each other. Kim Merritt and I talked a lot about training. Then we raced. Christa Vahlensieck won with 2:45:24. Kim came in second with 2:47:43. I came in third, 32 seconds behind Kim. I'll never forget coming across the finish line. Kim just came up and grabbed and hugged me. She was more happy for me than for herself."

At the New York City Marathon in 1976, Gayle and Ben met Jesse Bell, president of Bonne Bell cosmetics. He invited them to Cleveland, where the firm is located. Ben Barron soon was supervising Bonne Bell's series of 10,000-meter races for women, which in two years grew from three events to 24, in as many cities. Gayle ran in many of the races, which sometimes attracted fields of 3,000 or more runners, all women. Only a few years before, even men's races were not that big.

Gayle's increased race schedule, however, resulted in a pulled hamstring (her first serious injury). Beginning in January 1977 she did not race for six months, missing Boston. Recovered, she ran three marathons toward the end of the year: Eugene, Oregon (2nd in 2:48:34); New York (3rd in 2:52:19); and Honolulu (2nd in 2:51:18). Though consistent, she never had won a major marathon.

Tired from so many races, she cut her training through January 1978, averaging only five to eight miles a day. (Gayle never runs more than 80 miles a week.) Gayle was uncertain whether or not to run the Avon Women's International Marathon in her home town of Atlanta on March 19, 1978. Two months of solid training changed her mind. She finished fifth (2:53:05), but it took her a week to recover from the ill effects caused by heat and

The usual enthusiastic crowd at the start of the Boston Marathon
every year. (*Jeff Johnson*)

Bill Rodgers (number 14) with Canada's Jerome Drayton (number 5) close behind in the 1975 Boston Marathon. (*Jeff Johnson*)

Frank Shorter, the 1972 Olympic gold medalist, relaxing before a race. (*Jeff Johnson*)

Above left: Barefoot Garry Bjorklund running in the 10,000 meter race at the 1976 Olympic Trials in Eugene, Oregon. *(Jeff Johnson)* *Above right:* Bill Rodgers pacing himself in preparation for his win in the 1976 New York City Marathon. *Below:* Frank Shorter (number 2) leading in the First Chicago Distance Classic in 1977. *(Ray Boldt)*

Above left: Frank Shorter crossing the finish line in the 10,000 meter race at the 1976 Olympic Trials in Eugene, Oregon. *(Jeff Johnson)* *Above right:* Gayle Barron trains often with her husband Ben. *(Head Sports Wear) Below:* Gayle Barron (number 10) and Martha Cooksey (just behind and to the left of Gayle) among the leaders in the Avon International Marathon Championships for Women in March 1978, in Atlanta. *(Janeart, Ltd.)*

Gayle Barron (number 229) winning at the 1978 Boston Marathon. It wasn't until the last moment that Gayle decided to enter. (*Jeff Johnson*)

Bill Rodgers in a quietly contented moment after winning the 1977 Cleveland Heart-A-Thon. *(Peter Renerts)*

Martha Cooksey, a close contender with Grete Waitz, snatching a cup of water during the 1978 New York City Marathon. *(Manufacturers Hanover Trust, F. Charles)*

An aerial view of the Verrazano-Narrows Bridge at the start of the 1978 New York City Marathon. *(Manufacturers Hanover Trust, J. Mundy)*

An unusual traffic jam on the Verrazano-Narrows Bridge at the start of the 1979 New York City Marathon. Over 11,000 runners began this race. *(UPI)*

CROSSING

Bill Rodgers (right) about to take over Kirk Pfeffer (left) in the 1979
New York City Marathon. *(UPI)*

Bill Rodgers glancing back after overtaking Kirk Pfeffer in the 1979
New York City Marathon. *(UPI)*

Bill Rodgers crossing the finish line in record time in the 1979 New York City Marathon. *(UPI)*

Right and below: An elated Bill Rodgers and Grete Waitz as they share victory in the 1979 New York City Marathon, he for the fourth consecutive time, she for the second. *(UPI)*

hills. Only four more weeks remained before the Boston Marathon, and she did not attempt to enter.

But Ben planned to run. Gayle finally decided to go with him to watch the race. Four days before the race, Gayle decided to enter. She figured she could see the race as well from the inside as the outside.

Entries to the Boston Marathon had closed to most people a month earlier. But because Gayle was well-known and had run well at Boston before, the B.A.A. officials were happy to have her. They issued a special last-minute number. Women runners had come a long way from the time when Roberta Gibb Bingay had to leap out of the bushes in 1966.

Gayle Barron showed little concern over her performance. She was more interested in having fun. She brought only her training shoes to Boston, not the lightweight models she normally raced in. The morning of the race, Gayle breakfasted on raisin bread covered with peanut butter, not her usual pre-race meal.

While warming up behind the Hopkinton gym with Kim Merritt, Gayle became separated from Ben. The Barrons planned to meet, if separated, by the statue in Hopkinton Square near the starting line so they could run together. When Gayle arrived at the statue, however, it seemed as though everybody else was meeting their friends there too. So she went to the line without Ben. When the gun sounded, she was swept up in the excitement of the moment.

"I knew the moment I took the first step that I was feeling good," Gayle recalls. "When I got to five miles, I discovered my split was around 29:00. That was just *way* too fast for me. Normally I would have panicked, but I decided I'd just see how long I could hold a good pace."

At eight miles Gayle pulled even with Kim Merritt, something she never had done before. Kim's husband

Keith told her they were running at about a 2:37 or 2:38 pace. If they continued that fast, they would have broken Kim's American record.

The two women ran together, and by 14 miles caught Gayle Olinek of Canada, who had gone out fast and was fading. They soon left her behind. Gayle Barron noticed that Kim was not running as smoothly as usual, having had some problems with her tendons. Through the Newton Hills they jockeyed back and forth, one passing the other, until around 20 miles Kim no longer responded to the challenge. Surrounded by men, Gayle had no idea what position she then held among the women in the race.

"Kim and I weren't paying attention," Gayle recalls. "You can't with that kind of crowd. In an all-women's race you can look around and see where everybody was. But I really wasn't sure of my place. I knew I had to be close to the front when I passed Kim, but no one ever told me I was the first woman.

"They were screaming so loud that I couldn't hear anyway. It was like a thunder roar, and I've never heard crowds like that in my life. It was almost the most exciting experience I've ever had. You can't imagine the noise. It was almost to the point where you wanted to put your hands over your ears. As the people saw me coming, they would go crazy, especially toward the end of the race. I was thinking about the crowds, the excitement, and the fact that I knew I could do it, and was feeling better and better the closer I got to the end."

The moment Gayle Barron crossed the finish line she asked "Did I win?" But the noise was still so intense she could not hear. Then suddenly there were policemen surrounding her and they were leading her to the reviewing stand, so she thought, *I must have won!* Gayle Barron finished the first woman at Boston that day. Her time was 2:44:52, a personal record by nearly three minutes. Kim Merritt finished fourth in 2:47:52.

Ben, running with a cramped muscle, finished seven minutes later. He had not realized until two-thirds through the crowded race that his wife was running ahead of him, not behind him. Even when he crossed the line, Ben didn't know what had happened. "Who won?" he shouted at a woman standing near the chute.

"I think it was Kim Merritt," replied the woman.

But another spectator corrected her, "No, it was Gayle Barron."

Gayle by that time was standing on the victory stand, laurel wreath on her head. She dabbed at the tears cascading down her cheeks. It was a startling moment for a woman whose running career had consisted mostly of jogging a mile or two around a stadium track.

Gayle Barron vividly remembers that moment; "The crowds were still screaming. The excitement was like the Olympic Games. I was up on the victory stand, and it was like a dream fulfilled. Finally, after about three minutes, they asked me to get down. 'Rats,' I thought. I just wanted to stand up there forever. Three minutes! And those three minutes have to last a whole lifetime."

9
RUNNING THE LAKES

On a June evening, Garry Bjorklund ran down by the lakes. The evening was hot and humid, and Garry wore only rust-colored shorts and a pair of yellow running shoes. He sported a brush mustache. He ran lightly with a smooth stride.

Garry was training for the New York City Marathon later in the year. He had covered maybe a half mile from the apartment in the Uptown area of Minneapolis that he shares with his two roommates, Mike Slack and Brad Kingery. Mike and Brad ran with Garry on an eight-mile course that he uses frequently during a training program that sometimes hits 150 miles a week.

Mike Slack is a miler, a good one, although he also runs road races. He placed fifth in the 1976 American Olympic trials in the 1,500 meters and has a best time of 3:37 in that event. Brad Kingery is a distance runner who finishes well in local road races. Garry Bjorklund is one of the top 10,000 meter runners in the world, having made the finals in that event at the Montreal Olympics. In 1977 he switched to the marathon, running 2:13:46 in only his third race at that distance. Many people feel that Garry Bjorklund (who goes by the nickname "B. J.") is the American runner most likely to succeed Frank Shorter and Bill Rodgers to the title of King of the Road.

88

Mike and Garry train together almost daily. Brad tries to work out with them when he can. "Nobody else likes to run with these guys," admits Brad. "They train too hard."

That evening Mike and Garry had promised Brad to take an easy, relaxed run—a "repair" workout—but before long the pace began to edge near 6:00-per-mile. As though bored with even this snail-like pace, Mike moved off the path circling Lake of the Isles and splashed through the shallow water along the shore, shouting, "Quack! Quack! Quack!"

"You're scaring the ducks," Garry told him.

Mike darted out of the water and back up to the path, where a jogger approached. "Hello," he greeted the jogger with a smile.

"Now you're scaring the joggers," kidded Garry.

The pace of the workout continued to be fast. Mike and Garry chattered about anything and everything: girls, workouts, business, races, people. Their talk was light-hearted and friendly, with each roommate trying to make fun of the other. But Brad struggled to keep up with his roommate, and soon detoured onto another course, allowing his roommates to push on without him.

Mike Slack talked about their racing. "We like to go out hard," he commented on the strategy often employed by Garry and himself in distance runs. As to what they mean by "hard," Mike explained, "4:20 or better for the first mile. That's where our track background comes in. None of the road racers around the country like to go out hard. Rodgers is the only one." In a 10,000-meter road race held in Minneapolis two weekends before, Garry and Mike rolled past the mile in 4:13.

"That spread the field a bit," said Garry, a smile appearing beneath his brush mustache.

It is at moments such as this—running, when his

guard is down—that you get just a slight hint of what Donnie Timm, former teammate of Bjorklund at the University of Minnesota, refers to as Garry's "subtle cockiness."

Do not mistake that statement as critical of Garry's personality, since he is reserved, soft-spoken, almost gentle. He is a master of understatement. You could stand in a room for fifteen minutes with Garry Bjorklund and not realize he was there. You might talk to him for another fifteen minutes and not realize what he has accomplished as a runner. Yet he is not without strength. He also is not without ego.

Donnie Timm states: "It's not something Garry will ever verbalize, but he has this inner assurance that he's best. He's very quiet, very humble, but in the back of his mind he knows that he'll beat you any day of the week."

Roy Griak, track coach at the University of Minnesota, says of his former runner, "He's got a tough mind—like shoe leather."

Although he competes in a sport, long-distance running, that has been called "lonely," Garry Bjorklund has been described by Roy Griak as the complete team man. Once during cross-country season when Garry had a severe cold, Coach Griak spotted a turtleneck pullover in a discount store. He bought it for his star performer for less than two dollars. Garry refused to accept the turtleneck unless the other members of the team got one too.

Garry is independent and self-reliant. Donnie Timm says: "I always thought if Garry was drowning, he'd never ask for a life preserver. He'd rather flounder around until he got out on his own."

Moving away from the lake, Garry and Mike headed up a steep hill and the pace quickened. "We like to force the hills," commented Garry. They now moved through

90

Theodore Worth Park, a wooded area that includes trails, bike paths, a bird sanctuary, and lots of hills. Hills make runners tough.

They came down out of the park and crossed a bridge over the Great Northern railroad tracks, their feet sounding hollowly on the wooden planks. They moved through a residential area, along quiet side streets with few vehicles and no runners. Garry and Mike enjoy running here more than around the many scenic lakes of Minneapolis. The lakes are populated by too many dogs, bikers, and joggers. "On weekends it's like a zoo," claimed Mike. "You can't move."

"All the runners in Minneapolis are locked into the lakes," stated Garry.

Often on weekends the roommates travel to Anoka to run with Donnie Timm, a steeplechaser. Or they head north. "We know some dynamite trails," offered Garry. "We were running a place called Elm Creek one time and decided to go left instead of right. We got lost. We were running through briar patches, jumping over streams."

"Itch weed so bad we could hardly stand it."

"Best workout we ever had!"

Their run brought them back to the lake nearest their apartment. Garry and Mike slowed, then stopped. Garry began some stretching exercises. "I'm totally inflexible," he confessed, bending to reach barely below his knees. The two did some strides of about 100 yards in length, jogging between: two fast, two easy, two fast. They did them to improve their finishing kick.

Among the leading American road runners, Garry Bjorklund may possess the most natural speed, a talent carefully disguised because he goes out so hard he rarely needs to outkick anybody. Also, he seldom runs short distances on the track anymore. Garry ran 4:05 for the mile as a high school senior and 4:02.2 as a college freshman before his coach realized he had even more ability for longer distances.

Some of the track workouts Garry takes are almost legends among Minnesota runners. He sometimes runs a 30–40 drill, where he runs a 30-second 220, followed by a 40-second 220. The first time he tried it, he covered two-and-a-half miles at this fast-slow pace; on another occasion he went three.

Still another workout is to sprint a 110 down the straightaway, jog the turn, then keep repeating that pattern. The idea is to learn to surge in the middle of a race so nobody can surprise you with a sudden change in pace. One time Donnie Timm and Garry Bjorklund did a mile of 110 surges, and someone on the sideline clocked them in 4:20. Another time Garry did two miles of 110 surges, the total time being under 9:00. "Garry likes to bite off big challenges," states Donnie.

Garry also does his hard marathon training on a unique three-week cycle. In the first seven days, he and Mike cover 150 miles of mostly distance running: nine miles in the morning, 12 to 15 miles in the afternoon, much of it "very quick," according to Mike. "Of the 150 miles we did one week, 86 were under 5:30."

In the second seven-day period, they cut their mileage in half. They go only 70 miles, but doing more speed work in the parks or fast running on the track. It is almost as though, having trained one week at what Garry does best, they train a second week in Mike's specialty.

The third seven-day period combines the two previous styles of training. They cover 130 miles, but also include at least two speed sessions. Then they repeat the pattern the next three weeks, and the next, and the next. Any races run during this time are approached low-key as a form of fast training.

"Those are incredible weeks," says Mike Slack, slowly shaking his head. "You don't do much other than run. You float along day after day."

But it is the price that runners must pay if they want to be best in the world, particularly in the marathon.

10
THE KID FROM TWIG

Garry Bjorklund has come a long way from the day
when he first arrived in Minneapolis with manure
on his boots. His coach at the University of Minnesota,
Roy Griak, used to call Garry "The kid from Proctor with
the bowl haircut." Proctor is a town of 3,123 people just
west of Duluth, Minnesota.

But Proctor was the big city where Garry Bjorklund
attended high school, spending an hour and a half on
buses to get there. "I actually come from Twig," says
Garry, the smile on his face showing that even he is
amused by the fact.

Garry Bjorklund was born in Duluth, Minnesota,
on April 22, 1951. He grew up in that city, but his father
decided he wanted to be a farmer and bought forty acres
in Twig, about forty miles from Duluth. Bjorklund is a
Swedish name, the "j" being sounded as a "y," and you
almost need to live in the North Country to be able to
pronounce it properly. The Bjorklund farm had cows,
pigs, chickens, and a lot of land that Garry could roam
with a shotgun or fishing pole.

Garry was overweight when young. He displayed
little interest in competitive sports. He admits, "In grade
school we had thirteen kids in our class—ten boys and

94

three girls. To give you an idea how bad I was in sports, the girls would get chosen to play before I would. I just wasn't with it at all."

In seventh grade, however, Garry suddenly grew. He shed his baby fat, reaching 5 feet 9 inches and 130 pounds, only a few inches and pounds below his current size. He went out for track that spring, but lasted only two workouts. "I decided it was the dumbest thing I ever did in my life. All I liked to do was hunt and fish. Those were the two major sports in Minnesota."

Two larger boys who caught the same bus with Garry and his best friend, however, were athletes and they disliked his attitude. "The next fall when we didn't go out for football they beat us up. In the winter when we didn't go out for hockey they beat us up. When spring came around, I didn't want to get beat up again, so I decided to give track one more try."

Garry remembers that on his first day at practice, the coach sent them out for a six-mile run. Even though he was only in eighth grade, Garry beat everybody on the high school varsity except one boy. The next week they ran a nine-and-a-half mile workout and Garry beat even that one boy by a mile and a half. In an article that appeared in the local newspaper a few days later, the coach praised his gangly little eighth-grader for the achievement. "That really turned me on," Garry admits.

His progress in track was fast. The first time he ran a mile as an eighth-grader, he hit 4:52. He dropped that time to 4:42 by the end of the season. As a high school freshman, he ran 4:19 and placed third in the state. As a sophomore, junior, and senior, he won the state mile with respective bests of 4:14, 4:09, and 4:05.

That sounds impressive enough even by national standards, but in Minnesota winters are cold and the track season is so short as to be almost invisible. His achievement was phenomenal. Placing second behind him his senior year with 4:11 was Mike Slack. In almost any other area or in Minnesota at any other time, Mike would have been unbeaten. Mike recalls their final high school race, "We went out in 1:57 and I died. Garry died too, but a lap later."

Despite his current success running long distances, Garry Bjorklund had less luck in cross-country as a high schooler. He played football in the fall as a freshman, took sixth in the state cross-country meet both his sophomore and junior years, and finally won as a senior.

By that time college coaches from all over the country were approaching him with scholarship offers. Garry decided to stay in Minnesota and go to the state university to train under Roy Griak. According to Donnie Timm, "Everybody was approaching Garry telling him about all the places he would go *when* he made their team. Roy Griak kept talking about *if* he made the team. I think it was this extra challenge that most appealed to Garry."

Except for the second meet of the season, when he was hobbled by a knee injury after tripping during a workout, Garry Bjorklund went undefeated in dual meets his freshman year. He also won the Big Ten* title and placed fifth in the NCAA championships at Van Cortland Park in New York. Indoors he placed fourth in the NCAA two mile with 8:42.0. But Garry still considered himself a miler. He won the Big Ten-mile outdoors in 4:03.6 and did 4:02.2 winning the Central Collegiate championships. This time, run as a freshman in 1970, remains his personal record for that distance, because he soon would move upwards into longer and longer events.

"I sealed my own fate the week after the Big Ten meet," recalls Garry. "I had also won the three mile at the

*An athletic conference of major universities in the midwest.

Big Ten meet in 13:40, so my coach got me in the Kennedy Games in California. I ran against Shorter and Bacheler. They ran 13:13 and I ran 13:16. Steve Prefontaine of Oregon had only run 13:13 that year, so the coach decided to enter me in the three mile at the NCAA."

Garry placed third in the NCAA three mile. But later at the National AAU track and field championships, in that event he placed only sixth. "It was terrible," he recalls.

"After the race the coach said, 'They've got a six mile tomorrow—24 laps on the track—why don't you run it as a workout? It's not going to hurt you.' So I ran the six mile behind Shorter and Bacheler, got third place, and was on my way to Europe on an AAU tour. After that, there was no way I was going to get close to a mile again. It was three miles, six miles, all the time."

Bjorklund's time in that AAU race was 27:30.6, an NCAA record. That summer he ran 10,000 meters in 28:50.4 in both France and Germany. "Garry had a quality of naïveté when he came here as a freshman," recalls Roy Griak. "He didn't even think that there might be people better than he who might win. He didn't know there were guys like Shorter whom he would not be able to outkick in the last lap."

Donnie Timm, however, explains that part of that attitude was instilled by Griak. "The coach told Garry not to fear anyone, but to respect everybody. That's still true today. I don't think Garry is afraid of anyone, whether on the track or on the roads."

As a sophomore, Garry Bjorklund continued his unbeaten record. In cross country, he won the Big Ten meet again. But he came down with appendicitis two days later and missed the NCAA meet.

This was part of a pattern that plagued Garry during his collegiate career. He was rarely beaten by his opponents, but he sometimes was beaten by injuries. Some of these injuries were caused by his own drive. He wanted to train harder than his body could take.

Garry lost six weeks recovering from his appendicitis operation, but still came back to win the two mile at the Big Ten meet indoors with 8:49.0. At the NCAA indoor track meet a week later, however, he went unplaced.

Outdoors, Garry broke his NCAA six-mile record at the Drake Relays with 27:24.8, placing second behind Frank Shorter. He won that event in the NCAA meet in Washington with 27:43.1. Then he placed second in the AAU meet in Eugene, Oregon, with 27:28.2.

This qualified Garry for the Pan American Games in Cali, Colombia, later that summer.

"I was a real crowd-pleaser in Colombia," Garry recalls wryly. "Majia of that country caught me with 200 meters to go and passed me to get the bronze medal (behind Shorter and Martinez of Mexico). The place went crazy: 50,000 people chanting: 'Ma-hee-uh! Ma-hee-uh!' I never before felt so small or insignificant."

His fourth-place time on a hot day was 29:18.4. It disappointed him, but the following year he continued his undefeated dual meet record in cross-country, won the Big Ten meet for the third straight year, and lost only to Steve Prefontaine at the NCAA championships in Tennessee. "I thought I gave him a pretty good battle," says Garry with quiet pride. "That was probably my best race as a collegian."

With the Olympic Games scheduled the following summer of 1972, Garry Bjorklund seemed almost certain of making the American team. He might even be a medal winner. But his athletic career took a sudden turn downward. In January 1972 he accepted an invitation to run the three miles in Madison Square Garden at the Millrose

Games in New York. He placed third in 13:24.4, but afterward his foot hurt.

"Garry was elated when he returned from New York," recalls Roy Griak. "He had run well. Shorter had just nipped him. He took a track workout the next day, but he had a little limp and we cut the workout short. He was still limping one day later. The injury persisted. We had him checked by doctors, X-rayed, given cortisone shots, but nothing helped. He won the Big Ten three-mile indoors literally on one leg, but he couldn't practice. The doctors eventually decided that he had an extra novicular bone in one foot, and it would have to be removed surgically."

Thus Garry Bjorklund's Olympic chances for 1972 vanished almost overnight. He finished out the track season, getting beaten in the Big Ten meet. During the summer he quit running. While Frank Shorter was training for the Olympic marathon, which he won in Munich, Garry Bjorklund was sitting around gaining weight.

That fall he had an operation on his foot. He spent six months on crutches, then started jogging in May. But a few months later he got hurt again. While working on a construction job, he fell into a ditch and hurt his knee. It swelled up like a balloon, so he didn't run again until one week before the start of cross-country season. "I was twenty-two pounds overweight," says Garry. "It was bad, real bad."

When he injured his foot, the doctor had told Garry he never would run again. "That scared the dickens out of me," says Garry, "because I realized that as a junior in college I was about a quarter inch away from becoming a nobody."

During the period of his injury, Garry had pulled away from his teammates. He refused to go to their meets. He recalls: "For a while I went the route that most insecure people go. I messed around, partied all the time, and became something that I really wasn't. After about a year I started piecing it together and decided I could be just about anything I wanted if I was willing to invest."

Previously only a fair student, Garry Bjorklund began to concentrate on his studies. He improved his grade index from 2.5 to 3.5. But he still felt uncertain about his future as a runner and went out for cross-country in the fall of 1973 only because he was given a fifth year in college on scholarship.

At the beginning of the season, Garry ran so poorly he could not even make the Minnesota seven-man traveling squad. For someone who, except for the second meet his freshman year and national championship races, had gone undefeated in cross-country, it was a long way to descend. "I hated it. I really did," he admits. "I had to go out and eat crow every week."

Roy Griak records the times of all his athletes on yellow cards, and the record of Garry's senior year that fall was one of continued futility:

10/13 Michigan State	DNF*
10/20 Iowa	14th
11/26 Twin Cities Track Club	15th
11/3 Big Ten	37th
11/10 NCAA District	52nd
11/19 NCAA	147th

At the NCAA championships in Spokane, Washington, he was running far back in the pack when he overheard one runner behind him say to another: "Hey, there's Bjorklund. Let's take him!" And they did.

Indoor track was little better. In one meet in

*Did not finish.

January he ran the 880 in 2:05. At the Big Ten championships, he went unplaced in the two mile with 9:08.8.
Finally outdoors, he began to show signs of his previous
brilliance. He won the Texas Relays three mile with
13:39.9 and the Big Ten with 13:31.6. "It was a 'gimme.'
There were other runners who could have beaten me, but
somehow they all entered other events." Then at the
NCAA championships in Texas in June, on a hot and
humid evening, he failed to finish the six mile. It was a bad
end to his collegiate career and perhaps to his running
career.

"I came back to Minneapolis and had my bags all
packed," Garry recalls. "I was going to go back to Duluth
and be a farmer or something. But Donnie Timm had
qualified for the AAU meet in the steeplechase and wanted
me to stay and help him train for that meet. So I ran with
him a couple of times, and went out on a few runs of my
own, and talked to myself a little bit to try and work things
out.

"Then Coach Griak called and said there was a man
in town willing to pay my expenses to the AAU meet. I
figured, why not, one last hurrah, then call it a day. So I
went out to L.A., placed third, and ran my fastest 10,000
ever (28:28.4). That just blew me away. I couldn't figure it
out, because I was just so intent on quitting. I just didn't
want to do it anymore.

"I went back to Twig for two months, and while I
was there that summer, I thought about running even
though I didn't run a step. I used my energy to build a
garage. I went out and ordered the lumber. I put the
cement down myself and built that doggone garage. I
think every time I hit a nail I was kind of hitting myself.
And I thought about it, and thought about it, and talked
to my mother about it, and what I came up with was that I
didn't want to quit."

11
A BAREFOOT RUNNER

In the fall of 1974, Garry Bjorkland returned to
Minneapolis and took two jobs. During the day he
repaired lawnmowers. At night he delivered pizzas.

After Christmas he packed his bags and took a
Greyhound bus to Louisiana, where a friend had promised him a job. He arrived in Baton Rouge on December
29, 1974, with $17 in his pocket, to find that the promise
of a good job and good housing had been only that: a
promise.

"Part of the breakdown of the system with our
Olympians," comments Garry, "is that college is such a
protected environment. You're sheltered from the world.
When you get out in the real world and you say, 'Hey, I'm
somebody. I'm training for the Olympics,' People tell you,
'Who cares? What else can you do?' "

Garry borrowed some money from a friend. Finally
he got a job working at International House of Pancakes
for 90¢ an hour plus all he could eat. He worked for four
months, ran with the track team at Louisiana State University, and made some good friends. When he saved
enough money, Garry bought a '63 Rambler and decided
to leave town.

Garry did not want to come home from Louisiana a

failure, so he began to look for some place else to train. "I called a guy from California who once asked me to come out and run for his track club, and he said, *'Garry who?'* There was only one other guy that I knew in the whole country who lived where I thought I would get decent training."

The man was Kent Swenson, then assistant coach at the University of Colorado. "Kent, it's too hot here," said Garry when he called him. "I've got to get out of Louisiana."

"Come on out," said Swenson.

"Can I get a job?"

"No, but come on out anyway."

Garry Bjorklund moved to Boulder, Colorado. Ken Sparks, a former half miler from Ball State University, offered him a place to live for free. He soon got a job as a janitor.

Several other runners shared a three-bedroom trailer house: Brad Kingery, Fred Carnihan of Nebraska, and Ted Castaneda of Colorado. Garry moved in with them and soon was joined by Mark Weeks and Charlie Vigil. Garry wrote Mike Slack, who moved out from Minnesota, then Marv Johnson of Maryland arrived, followed by several more. "We had eleven runners living in a three-bedroom trailer house," says Garry. "Nobody had a good job. Nobody cared. We were just training our heads off. Any time of the day, if you wanted to go for a run, there was somebody to do it with. The best chess games in the world. Everybody shared everything. Making the Olympic team was important, but other things along the way were more important."

In the summer of 1975 at the Pan American Trials, Garry won the 10,000 meters and Mike Slack won the 5,000 meters. At the games in Mexico City, Garry Bjorklund placed fourth as he did in Colombia in 1971.

He was back where he had been, a strong bet to make the Olympic team—but he had lost four years.

Then at the Olympic Trials in Eugene, Oregon, in 1976, tragedy again struck. Only three runners could qualify for the team in each event. In the 10,000 meters he was running against Frank Shorter, Bill Rodgers, and Craig Virgin, an NCAA champion from the University of Illinois.

Garry was cruising along comfortably in the middle of the pack when somebody accidentally stepped on his foot. It caused him to lose one of his track shoes.

Garry relates what happened: "I was cruising along and everything was good," he begins. "You know when you're really fit and you're tuned into something. The ankles feel good, the legs are good, traffic isn't too heavy, the temperature is mild, and everything is going well.

"At the corner of the track near the scoreboard, all of a sudden—*slap*—the shoe was gone! It was just like a hand came out of heaven and—*phttttt*—it was gone! The heel tab tucked underneath and I grabbed at that devil, but there was no way I could get the shoe back on. I ran about 75 to 100 yards and realized that the shoe was going to remain that way unless I stopped, so I kicked it off.

"At first I had a wild dash of hope that everything was going to be all right. But when you lose a shoe on the track, you realize in a hurry that your whole rhythm and flow is dependent on having that spike there. It helps you with your landing and your pull-through and your power-off on the next stride. Take away one of those shoes and the foot comes down, but it doesn't lock to the track. It kind of skids, so you get a little shuffle. It took me about 200 more yards to realize that I wasn't going to make the Olympic team. There was no way.

"Then I came around the corner again where I lost the shoe, and it was near the athlete's section. A couple of
104

the athletes were sitting up in the stands. They saw the shoe was gone, so they shouted, 'Hey, dude. Don't give up. Hang in there!' So I figured, heck, what have I got to lose?

"I ran another lap and came around to that corner, and about 25 people this time were shouting at me, 'Come on, gol-dang it!' I came around again, and there were 75 people pulling for me. Next lap, 150. Then 300. And 500. Every time I came around, the group just got bigger and bigger and yelled a little louder, and finally with two laps to go it caught on with the main straightaway side of the stadium. By that time there were 7,000 people into the event.

"With two laps to go Shorter, (Craig) Virgin, and Rodgers just ran away from me, and I thought again, 'No way.' But after another 50 yards Rodgers faltered a little. I don't know why, sometimes you can sense it, but I knew. I went down the main straightaway and people were going bananas. I got on the back straight and people were on their feet yelling—and Rodgers was coming back to me.

"It seemed as though the harder I wished, the more he came back. Then with 200 yards to go, I lost all feeling. I lost all my senses except a tempo with the crowd: 'rah-rah-rah!' It was as though all their energy was funneled right into me. I had water coming out of my eyes. Crazy! And when I hit the finish line in third place, I couldn't believe it. I made the Olympic team! It was the first time in my life I ran a victory lap. It was really sweet!

"For three days afterward, I couldn't sleep. At the end of the day I would lay in bed, look at the ceiling, and start to smile. I would go out for a run and people would drive by and give me a funny look, and I realized, here I am running down the road with a big grin on my face. It wasn't real."

It took some time for Garry Bjorklund to descend to earth after the thrill of making the Olympic team. One day (actually after the games), he visited a friend's sixth-grade class and brought some of his shoes, his medals, his clippings, and talked about the experience of making the team. Afterward one of the children asked: "Hey, how many guys go to the Olympics?"

"Just three in each event," said Garry, trying to impress on the child the importance of the trials.

"Which one were you?"

"I was third."

The child thought a moment, then said: "Ahhh, you scabbed in!"

The dream of having qualified for the Olympics faded into the reality of having to compete against runners the caliber of Finland's double gold medalist, Lasse Viren. Among those rooming with Garry Bjorklund in Montreal was Craig Virgin. Garry had won three straight Big Ten cross-country titles, then Craig came along to win *four*.

A strong rivalry exists between Craig and Garry. On the day officials posted the draw for the 10,000 heats, Craig returned to the room and smiled at Garry, "Wait until you see the heat you got."

Garry went downstairs to look at the bulletin board and gulped. He had some of the fastest runners in his heat: Viren, Puttemans, Quax, Hernandez, and Simmons. Only three from each heat advanced to the finals, plus the three fastest non-placers. Only one or two other runners had times slower than Garry. "I figured in two days I would run, go out and have a good try, and that would be the Olympics," he says.

In the 10,000 meter heat, Tony Simmons of England started fast and broke loose from the field. At four miles Lasse Viren, the defending champion, was floating along behind Chris Wardlaw of Australia and

106

Emil Puttemans of Belgium. That threesome surged and soon had 50 yards on Bjorklund, who was on the verge of being eliminated.

But with five laps to go, Wardlaw grew wary of setting the pace for Viren and Puttemans. He slowed and moved wide to force Viren to take the pace. Viren refused to accept the challenge, and the pace slowed so much that Bjorkland caught them in the space of one straightaway. Garry did not hesitate and actually blew by them on the inside. Simmons still was far ahead.

Garry pushed the next four laps at what he described as merely a "good tempo." When he looked back with one lap to go, he was surprised to see that the others had failed to stay with him. Tony Simmons won the heat. Garry ran 28:10 in the second place and qualified for the finals in what was the fastest of all the heats. The other two Americans, Virgin and Ed Mendoza, failed to advance. (Although Frank Shorter qualified for the 1976 Olympics at 10,000, he decided to pass that event for the marathon, where he won a silver medal for second, to go with his gold from Munich.)

"I was sky-high after my heat," recalls Garry. "I felt so pumped that if twenty minutes later they said do it again, I'm sure I could have run as fast, or faster. But the next day the edge started to wear off. The day after that, it wore down more. The night before the finals, I couldn't sleep. I don't think it helped having Virgin for a roommate, because he was so down. I woke up the morning of the finals and I don't think I was ready to go out and even run a 4:30 mile, much less face the best in the world. I shouldn't have been there, and those guys just took me apart."

Halfway through the 10,000-meter final, the tempo was pretty slow. Then Carlos Lopes of Spain surged.

107

Garry was running in fourth place at that time and he went with the other runner for a full mile until Lopes surged even faster. Garry started to fade. People began to boo him. He finished 13th.

But with the experience behind him, he already began to look forward to 1980 and Moscow. He returned to Minneapolis to start a sports store. He, Mike Slack, and Brad Kingery are partners in Garry Bjorklund Sports.

Indoors in 1977, Garry ran 13:07 for three miles. He raced in Trinidad, then in Japan, but suffered an ear infection that severely limited his training that spring. At the National AAU track and field meet outdoors, he dropped out of the 5,000 and failed to place in the 10,000.

Returning home dejected, he received a phone call from Duluth soon after to come run in Grandma's Marathon. Having nothing better to do that weekend, Garry agreed to do it. He ran 2:21:50 in 82-degree heat, then traveled 300 miles to southern Minnesota the next day to win an eight-mile road race.

Previously, Kenny Moore had been trying to convince Garry that he was wasting his time at 10,000 meters and might be better suited for the marathon. It was the same advice that Kenny had given Frank Shorter a half dozen years earlier. About that time a young boy appeared at Garry's store with a collection of old *Track & Field News* and about fifty different books on running. Garry bought the miniature library for $150, sat down and read everything he could about road running, and decided that he was going to become a marathoner.

Garry began to train for the 1977 New York City Marathon. In that race, Bill Rodgers began a surge around 15 miles that gradually carried him and Garry away from the rest of an eight-man pack. At 18 miles Garry, who had little experience drinking while running,

108

grabbed for a cup of liquid. It was too sweet. He gagged. A mile further down the road he vomited. Garry placed fifth in 2:15:14, but two months later won the Maryland Marathon with 2:13:46, breaking Bill Rodgers' record.

That time over a very demanding course seems to have impressed some of Garry Bjorkland's rivals more than him. "The other runners talk about what that effort would translate into on a flatter course, making it sound much better, but I don't think the race was that difficult. I think it was a 2:13 marathon, and that's all the emphasis I put on it. If others want to think it translates to 2:11 or 2:10, let them think it. To me, it's 2:13, and I've got to work to get a 2:10."

12
THE NEW YORK CITY MARATHON

Garry Bjorklund hoped to run his first 2:10 marathon in New York City on October 21, 1978. Bill Rodgers, the New York City winner the two previous years would be there, as would Frank Shorter and the third member of the 1976 American Olympic marathon, Don Kardong of Spokane, Washington.

Among the 10,000 expected starters were more than a thousand women. They included Christa Vahlensieck of West Germany, who held the women's marathon world record with 2:34:48, and Martha Cooksey of California, winner of the Avon Women's International Marathon in Atlanta in the spring. Cooksey announced her intention of breaking Vahlensieck's record.

Gayle Barron, however, did not plan to run New York. She passed it to run another marathon in New Zealand.

The first marathon run ever held in the United States was in New York, held even before the 1897 Boston Marathon, usually considered the oldest such race. This first American "marathon" in the fall of 1896 actually covered 35 miles between Stamford, Connecticut, and midtown Manhattan. It finished at Columbus Circle, on the southeast corner of Central Park. Of the thirty

110

entrants, only nine finished. *The New York Times* reported spectator reaction: "There was a pandemonium of joy . . . and women who knew only that the first race of its kind ever held in this country was nearing a finish waved their handkerchiefs and fairly screamed with excitement."

The race did not continue, however, and Boston went on to capture the attention of runners across the world. Marathoning died in popularity during the period between the two world wars, and in the 1950s there were only two or three full-distance marathons contested in the United States other than Boston.

One of these was the Yonkers Marathon in a suburban location just north of New York City. For several decades it served as the site for the National AAU Marathon Championship, and on occasion was one of the races used to determine which marathoners would represent the United States in the Olympic Games. Held toward the end of May, Yonkers had a rugged, hilly course. It seldom attracted much more than a hundred runners.

Other American marathons that began to develop around this time included the Western Hemisphere Marathon in Culver City, California, and the Heart of America Marathon in Columbia, Missouri. Even by 1960 such races were considered successes if a dozen or more runners appeared. Sports reporters paid them little attention, noticing each year only the winner at Boston, and sometimes not even that.

Meanwhile, a small group calling itself the New York Road Runners Club started a marathon, the Cherry Tree Marathon, within the city limits of New York. The race started in the Bronx near Yankee Stadium and wound four times around a lap course next to the Harlem River and the Major Deegan Expressway. The race was run in February when runners had to battle the weather, often snowy or a cold drizzle. They dodged around dere-

111

lict cars dragged off the expressway and abandoned nearby.

One of the runners who competed in the Cherry Tree Marathon in 1969 was Fred Lebow, an émigré from Austria and a textile consultant. A man in his forties, Lebow ran the race in a time of 4:20, so had ample time to think about the event, which he considered dreary and uninspired.

"The race wasn't supported by any city agencies," recalls Lebow. "Traffic was a problem, and the course went through some desolate areas. I remember kids throwing rocks at us along the route. And there was no reception for the hundred or so entrants after the race."

At about the same time, Mayor John V. Lindsay closed Central Park to automobile traffic on weekends to permit joggers, walkers, and cyclists freedom of movement. Lebow reasoned that the pleasant setting of Central Park with its trees, lakes, lawns, and rocky knolls would be an ideal marathon setting.

He suggested that the Road Runner Club use Central Park for its marathon the following year. He also wanted them to hold it in the fall when the weather is better for running.

The first New York City Marathon on September 13, 1970, attracted 166 runners, 72 of whom finished, led by Gary Muhrcke in 2:31:38. There was a single female competitor, Nina Kuscsik, a nurse at Mount Sinai Hospital. At that time the AAU refused to sanction female marathoners. Unfortunately, Nina seemed to justify their rebuke by her performance. Bothered by the flu, she failed to finish. (Nina would win the women's division in 1972 and 1973 and also be the first official women's winner at Boston in 1972.)

By 1972 Fred Lebow hoped to upgrade the level of the New York City Marathon by getting sponsors to provide money. He approached General Motors, who had just completed an office building on Fifth Avenue near Central Park. Lebow offered to bring the race out of Central Park and finish it next to the office building if they would provide $2,000 in sponsorship funds. General Motors decided that the marathon was not worth that much.

Six years later in 1978, Fred Lebow looked back on that decision with amusement. By then the budget of the New York City Marathon had grown to $350,000, with Manufacturers Hanover Bank contributing $125,000 of that sum for the right (among other considerations) to have its name on the numbers worn by nearly 10,000 entrants in what had become the world's largest marathon race.

Several factors combined to cause the New York City Marathon, within the span of a few years, to pass the Boston Marathon in numbers and rival it in prestige. Most important was the emergence in popularity of long-distance running as a sport. People who started by jogging one or two miles every other day at a gentle pace soon discovered they liked it. They enjoyed the feeling of being physically fit. They started running more and more, and some of them began to enter long-distance races. They seemed less interested in winning those races and beating other runners than they were in having a good time. They competed against themselves, measuring their success against their own previous times for different distances.

In 1978 the Gallop Poll estimated that 25 million Americans were jogging. While only a fraction of that number were "runners" who competed in races, more and more people had begun to enter marathons. The number of marathons in the United States grew to several hundred.

The number of people competing in the New York

City Marathon kept increasing: 535 in 1975, with 44 of them female. Because of this growth, Fred Lebow feared that the New York Road Runners Club must abandon its four-lap Central Park course. Since the fast runners lapped some of the slow runners several times, it was difficult to spot the leader or keep track of how far everybody went.

In 1976 the New York Road Runners Club obtained permission from the city government to start the race far across town. By then, the two-mile-long Verrazano-Narrows Bridge had been built across the mouth of the Hudson linking Staten Island (one of the city's five boroughs) with the rest of New York. The new marathon course would start on Staten Island, cross the bridge, and touch the other four boroughs: Brooklyn, Queens, the Bronx, and Manhattan. The finish line would be in Central Park.

By following this course the race would pass through different ethnic neighborhoods: Latin, Black, Italian, Polish, Jewish, and many others. It would give New Yorkers, and runners from out of town, a view of America's largest city while running through it. It would become a mammoth undertaking involving 800 policemen closing 350 intersections to prevent traffic from bothering the runners.

Twenty-eight gallons of blue paint would be required to paint a single blue line along the entire course. Marathoners would follow this blue line on their way from the Verrazano-Narrows Bridge to Central Park. In doing so, they would pass twenty-two water stations where 75,000 paper cups would be used to hand them water and other liquids. Almost overnight, the New York City Marathon had grown to become the biggest running event in the world.

Because of its size and importance, it also attracted

114

the world's greatest runners. In 1976 Bill Rodgers dueled Frank Shorter. Two months earlier in the Olympic marathon, Rodgers, bothered by an injury, had faded badly while Shorter won the silver medal. But by New York, Rodgers had recovered. Bill won with 2:10:09, ahead of Shorter with 2:13:11.

The following year, Garry Bjorklund, running in only his second marathon, challenged Rodgers for nearly twenty miles of the race. Then stomach cramps forced Garry to slow. He faded to fifth with 2:15:16 as Bill went on to record 2:11:28. Canada's Jerome Drayton placed second in 2:13:52.

For the 1978 race, Garry vowed to challenge Bill once again. Frank Shorter entered also, but did not expect to run with the leaders. A series of injuries had plagued Frank during the previous few years. He pulled a hamstring muscle while running a 10,000-meter race in Zurich the previous summer, an injury that caused him to drop out of the 1977 New York City Marathon.

He recovered slowly and the following spring needed an operation to remove a bone spur formed on his foot. Frank could not run for several months and maintained his conditioning mostly by working out on a stationary bicycle. He began running again during the summer and entered New York only to test his condition, with no hope of winning.

But the story at New York in 1978 was not so much Bill or Garry or Frank, but the total of 11,142 runners who registered for the race. (Of this number, 9,875 picked up their numbers and presumably started.) This number included 4,005 men who stated on their entry blank that they never had entered a marathon before. It also included 1,134 women. Sixty-seven city buses were used to transport many of these runners to the staging area at Fort Wadsworth, an Army installation near the Staten

115

Island side of the Verrazano-Narrows Bridge. Other runners hired taxicabs or arrived via private car.

One of those arriving in this manner was defending champion Bill Rodgers, who came with his wife Ellen in a limousine hired by a friend. He arrived an hour before the race start. Garry Bjorklund arrived about the same time, along with his business partner and roommate, Mike Slack. Gary and Mike had stayed overnight at the New York Athletic Club and traveled to the start in one of the two buses hired by the NYAC for its members running the race.

A small gym near the starting line was jammed with runners sitting or lying on the wooden floor. The day was warm, with the sun shining clearly in the sky overhead. (The Weather Bureau forecast temperatures in the seventies.) Most of the runners took advantage of the warm weather to relax outside on the grass. A marching band played for their entertainment.

But, although the warm weather made it pleasant waiting for the start and guaranteed a large number of spectators watching along the course, marathoners do not like warm weather while they run. Warm weather means they can overheat. Their body will sweat to cool down. They will need to drink liquids as they run to replace lost moisture. If they lose too much, their body temperature may rise. They could suffer from heat exhaustion. So while the runners enjoyed the warm weather before the start, they also realized that it could cause them problems before they reached Central Park.

Many other problems could arise during the running of 26 miles 385 yards. If they ran the first part of the race too fast, they might run out of energy and be unable to finish. Their muscles might cramp. They could suffer blisters on their feet that would bring them to a halt. The road to Central Park was rough, uneven, and lined with potholes, and a wrong step could cause a twisted ankle. Yet, despite these apparent hazards, 8,750 of the 9,875 starters, or 88.6 percent would finish. Most of those who crossed the finish line in Central Park, no matter how far behind, would have smiles on their faces, having won their own battle against fatigue.

The victory that each person achieves over himself in finishing 26 miles 385 yards is one reason why people run marathons, but at that moment Bill Rodgers was more concerned with achieving a personal victory over Garry Bjorklund and the other world-class runners in the race.

In addition to Rodgers, Shorter, Kardong (the three American Olympic marathoners from 1976), and Bjorklund (Olympic 10,000-meter finalist), the entry list also included Ian Thompson, who ran 2:09:12 to win the British Commonwealth Games Marathon in 1974. Injuries had limited Thompson's achievements since then, but he reportedly was back in top shape.

Also in the field was Lasse Viren of Finland, winner of the 5,000-and 10,000-meter runs in the 1972 and 1976 Olympics and fifth-place marathon finisher in 1976. Viren, however, seemed to be taking the New York City Marathon lightly and had come mostly to see the city. But any one of a number of other runners from Poland, New Zealand, Turkey, and other countries could surprise.

Fifteen minutes before the 10:30 A.M. start of the race, the grassy field at Fort Wadsworth began to empty as runners moved toward the starting line on the approach to the bridge. A few stragglers used the several dozen portable toilets or took a last sip of liquid at the refreshment table before rushing to the start. Garry Bjorklund was one of these. He and New Zealand's Kevin Ryan stood waiting for an open toilet inside the gym until the last minute.

For the first time, the New York City Marathon had

two starting lines: one on the left for women and runners in their first marathon, and one on the right for men with prior marathon finishes. Each group would cross the bridge on a different side and eventually merge several miles farther along the course.

There were several reasons for the dual start. It allowed a wider starting area, permitting runners to get closer to the starting line. At Boston that year, the number of competitors was so great that it took the trail runners six minutes to cross the starting line *after* the gun sounded. That penalty time would be reduced in New York to about one minute because of a broader line.

But a second and perhaps more important reason for the dual start was that it permitted all the women runners to start together. At Boston that year Penny DeMoss started in the middle of a group of men. Although she finished in second only a half minute behind Gayle Barron, Penny never saw Gayle during the race or knew where she was. At New York, the top female runners would be able to race each other over the first two miles. At least they could get some idea of their relative positions before joining, and being swallowed by, the faster male field.

In the last minute before the scheduled 10:30 start, the runners milled in front of the starting line. Race director Fred Lebow called over the loudspeaker for them to get back across the line. He worried that they might not be able to start the race on time. In response to his plea, the runners began to push back behind the line.

One who seemed relaxed was Frank Shorter. "I'm just going to run an easy pace and see how I feel," he announced to another runner who wished him good luck. Nevertheless, Frank still was very exact about his preparations. He had taken a scissors and trimmed every last piece of extra material from around the number four on

118

his chest, as though he could not bear the slightest extra weight. In deference to the sponsoring Manufacturers Hanover Bank, who had contributed $125,000 to the race budget, he carefully trimmed around their name on the number.

Bill Rodgers seemed less relaxed, the worry of winning the race for the third straight year weighing heavily upon him. He also was disturbed. Everything seemed slightly disorganized because of the large entry. Bill was looking the other way at 10:31 A.M. when the gun suddenly sounded, taking him by surprise. "Bang! And everybody was gone," Bill would comment later. "It seems to be a harder race each year."

13
"YOU'VE GOT TO HOOF IT"

The horde of nearly 10,000 runners swept across the Verrazano-Narrows Bridge. Two dozen helicopters, like bees around a hive, circled above and around the tall towers and cables of the bridge. Some of these helicopters contained reporters and photographers from newspapers, magazines, and TV stations. Others contained spectators who had paid $75 each for this view of the race.

Victor Mora of Colombia led up the incline of the bridge, accompanied by Barry Brown of Gainesville, Florida, and one other runner from Argentina. Barry was a 3:58 miler and 2:16 marathoner who wore the number 6011, mainly because he had entered too late to be issued one of the low numbers given to runners according to fast times.

He did not plan to finish the race, nor did Marty Liquori, a 3:52 miler who also lived in Gainesville. Both Marty and Barry had come to town to give a clinic for a running-shoe company at Macy's Department Store two days before. At the last minute, they decided to run the first fifteen or twenty miles of the marathon as their regular Sunday-morning long workout. Barry warned many of the fast runners of his plans so they would not get

120

worried if they noticed him running with them during the first ten miles. He, Mora, and the Argentinian passed the first mile in 5:02—fast, but not excessively fast for such a quality field. Garry Bjorklund was surprised that there was no mad rush for the lead as there had been the year before. Perhaps it was the warm weather, he thought.

As they moved onto the down slope of the bridge, a pack of several dozen runners engulfed the lead three. Moving to the front was Ian Thompson, clad in white shorts and vest with red, white, and blue bars across the chest, the British national uniform. He wore the number "one," identifying him as having the fastest time (2:09:05) of those entered.

Wearing the number "two" was another Englishman, Ron Hill, who had run his fastest time of 2:09:28 nearly a decade earlier. Ron won the Boston Marathon in 1971 in a record time. (Bill Rodgers had bettered Hill's Boston time when he ran his all-time best of 2:09:55, which earned him the third number.) Now forty years old, Ron Hill trailed the lead runners and hoped only to run faster than 2:20. Frank Shorter had the fourth fastest mark with 2:10:45, but he too planned an easy, steady pace. Frank made no attempt to go with the front runners.

By the time the lead runners came off the bridge, they had covered nearly two miles and passed from the borough of Staten Island to the borough of Brooklyn. Garry Bjorklund now had a slight lead with Englishman Chris Stewart on his left and training partner Mike Slack on his right.

Mike had a best time for the mile of 3:56 and finished fifth in the American Olympic trials 1,500 meters in 1976, but he had failed to finish either of the two previous marathons he had run. Just behind Mike and to his right was Ron Tabb, who was running with the leaders

121

despite having a previous best of only 2:22:02. He would fade and finish well back in 150th place with 2:37:27. Meanwhile, Bill Rodgers ran comfortably in the middle of the lead pack, content to save his sprint for later.

Around three miles Ian Thompson spurted ahead, gaining thirty yards on the rest of the leaders, which included Rodgers, Bjorklund, and Mora. They allowed Ian that much, but no more. For several miles the Englishman held the same thirty-yard lead. "I just watched him," Bill Rodgers said later. "I checked him," commented Garry Bjorklund. Kevin Ryan of New Zealand moved past Ian Thompson at one point, but then dragged back.

At seven miles Ian slowed slightly and the pack suddenly came together. This made Garry Bjorklund uncomfortable. "I get nervous when there are too many people around me," he says. "I looked over at Barry Brown and I didn't think he'd be there at the end. The Colombian was laboring. I said to myself, 'these guys shouldn't be here.' I wanted something to happen."

Around eight miles they passed through downtown Brooklyn and under the tower of the Williamsburgh Savings Bank, which they had seen on the horizon while running down Fourth Avenue for most of the last few miles. Coming through a series of short hills, Garry began to press the pace. Only Bill Rodgers went with him.

Bill thought Garry was crazy to make his move so soon. The day was hot, and Bill feared they might kill each other off. But he also feared giving Garry too great a lead. He might never catch him. So Bill Rodgers accepted the fast pace, but moved to a position two or three strides immediately behind. He wanted Garry to realize that the fast pace was of his choosing. Bill would do nothing to help.

At ten miles, a truck carrying photographers passed the two runners. On the back of the truck was Ellen

Rodgers, Bill's wife. Bill was about to raise his finger to his head and twirl it, indicating he thought Garry was nuts, but realized that the sun was at their backs. His shadow was running beside Garry's shadow. Garry might see the shadow of him making the sign. Bill did nothing, but kept hanging on.

When Garry took the lead, he hoped to push the pace hard to the Queensboro Bridge at 15 miles. But coming across the Pulaski Bridge two miles before, Garry began to weaken. They passed 13.1 miles, the halfway point, in 1:05, nearly fast enough to break Bill's course record despite the warm weather. Garry realized he had not been taking enough liquids. He slowed slightly.

Bill pulled even with Garry and for the first time in nearly five miles of hammering away at each other they spoke. "Are you all right?" Bill asked.

"I don't feel so good," replied Garry.

"Me either. What do you say we coast for a while?"

When the other runner agreed, Bill realized he probably had Garry beat. In the meantime, they could run together helping each other. Bill was not so sure about those running behind them. He worried that someone else would come up from behind.

The most likely person at that point would seem to be Don Kardong, who has a history of starting slow and finishing strong. At the 1976 Olympic marathon trials, the runner from Spokane, Washington, had come on in a rush over the last few miles to place third behind Shorter and Rodgers. Then in the Olympic marathon, Don used the same tactic and placed fourth, missing the bronze medal only by seconds.

At this stage in the New York City Marathon, Don Kardong ran with the pack trailing the two leaders. Several hundred yards separated him from the front, a short margin in a marathon. But he had not felt good from the

123

start. The pace seemed fast, but he heard no times. Don saw an occasional mile marker attached to a lamppost, but since he wore no watch could not tell how fast he was going. Someone called out his time at nine miles, but it meant nothing to him.

"I was up in about eighth place at the halfway point," Don Kardong recalled later. "I was almost up with Jack Foster of New Zealand. It was the last time that I felt even halfway good." Don Kardong began to slow down. He would not rush from behind for victory that day.

In the meantime, Garry Bjorklund was starting to struggle. He and Bill Rodgers reached the Queensboro Bridge running together as they had in the same race one year before. They started up the sidewalk of the mile-long bridge, on which had been laid a carpet, billed as "the longest carpet in the world." The carpet was laid over the bridge's steel grating to protect the runners' feet. But both Bill and Garry felt the carpet was too soft and ran on the grating anyway.

As they moved across the bridge beneath heavy, steel support girders, Bill began to push the pace. For the first time in the race Garry started to drop back. Bill's lead grew to ten yards, then thirty, then fifty.

During the race the front runners had been paced by several buses and trucks carrying reporters and photographers. There were helicopters overhead. Now and then one of the helicopters would drop down near the ground for their rotary blades, kicking up a tornado of dust. This bothered Bill since the dust got in his nose and under his contact lenses.

But crossing the Queensboro Bridge, Bill Rodgers glanced to his left and saw one of the helicopters moving even with him. Inside the helicopter was Arthur Klonsky, covering the race for *The Runner* magazine. Confident that he was running well at this point, Bill waved at Klonsky.

124

The photographer snapped a photo which appeared on the cover of that magazine.

Bill Rodgers made three left turns coming down off the bridge and ran under it and north along First Avenue. Garry Bjorklund trailed now by more than a hundred yards. After a gap of several hundred more yards, Trevor Wright of Great Britain appeared. He had passed his countryman Ian Thompson going across the bridge. Mike Slack was running fifth at this point, but he soon dropped out.

Meanwhile Frank Shorter had begun to increase his pace. Frank was running what for a runner of his talents was an easy pace. He had gone past the mile in 5:10 and hit five miles in 26:30. The rhythm did not feel right to him, so he had eased back. He passed the halfway point in 1:10, nearly a mile behind Rodgers and Bjorklund. He was in 65th place and no threat to the leaders, but he felt comfortable for the first time since his foot surgery. He also had begun to pass many of the runners who had gone out too fast and were dropping back.

Coming toward the Queensboro Bridge, Frank came along a stocky runner with dark hair. The other runner glanced across at Frank, seemed startled, and sped up as though unwilling to let him pass. Frank thought it strange that the other runner would expend so much energy in a personal duel at that point. The other runner would move ahead, then Frank, running a steady pace, would catch him causing the other runner to spurt again.

They turned onto the Queensboro Bridge, passing the fifteen-mile mark. The other runner finally turned to Shorter and said: "Balli."

"Oh," responded Frank. "Turkey." The other runner was Veli Balli of Turkey, who had a fastest time of 2:11:30. He had placed second in the Boston Marathon in 1977 behind Jerome Drayton of Canada. Frank Shorter

125

realized that if he was running even with Veli Balli at this stage in the New York City Maraton, he must not be doing too badly.

Coming off the Queensboro bridge, Barry Brown wanted to stop, but could not find a place to do so. After running the first ten miles hard, he slowed his pace waiting for Marty Liquori to catch him. Marty actually had climbed onto one of the bridge barriers near the start to watch the runners pass before joining them. Barry planned to meet Marty on the other side of the Queensboro Bridge, then run back to their hotel in time to see the finish. But Marty was nowhere in sight and Barry could not get off the course. "The spectators were shoulder to shoulder," said Barry, "and five and six deep. So I just kept running."

Bill Rodgers also kept running. Once off the bridge he relaxed slightly, feeling that he had covered the toughest part of the course. Despite police barricades, spectators crowded onto First Avenue, tightening the road on which he ran to a narrow alley. The crowd screamed encouragement at him and some of them touched him and patted him on the back as he passed. Children held out their hands for him to slap them. It sometimes seemed as though he were running straight into a wall of people, but as he grew nearer the wall would part, allowing him room to pass. He tried not to allow the crowd to distract him. He still might be caught from behind. He passed eighteen miles in 1:28:28, an average of 4:54 per mile. Now that he was running alone, however, his pace began to fall below a 5:00 average.

Several miles behind Bill Rodgers, Martha Cooksey of California ran surrounded by men. Marty was the lead woman runner, even though there were several hundred men ahead of her. A steady roar of cheers greeted all the runners passing down First Avenue, but the roar increased to a crescendo as the crowds recognized the lead woman runner.

Marty tried to listen for a second roar behind her which might hint the closeness of the second woman runner, but she could hear nothing. One of the men running beside her looked over his shoulder and announced, "There's nobody behind you."

But the man was wrong. He failed to spot Grete Waitz because she was moving up so rapidly. Grete wore red shorts and a white tank top with red and blue bars cutting sideways across it, symbolic of the Norwegian flag.

Suddenly Grete caught Marty and in an instant had a ten-yard lead on her. One of the men running beside Marty Cooksey said, "She's just surging. Don't let her get away." Marty increased her pace and moved three yards ahead of Grete.

But it was more than a mere tactical surge. Grete Waitz was a world-class track athlete who had won the women's international cross-country title that spring. Running in her first marathon and never having covered more than eighteen miles in training, she had started slowly. As the race went on, her confidence grew, so she began to increase her pace. She was moving much faster than Marty Cooksey at this point in the race and soon left her well behind. Marty started to slow down, her hopes of victory and a world record destroyed.

Up ahead, Garry Bjorklund maintained a steady pace up First Avenue, still in second place, but he was in trouble. His legs were beginning to cramp. He slowed to a jog, walked, and started running again. He was surprised that nobody had passed him yet. At twenty-one miles he left the course and sat down in a park. Some kids brought him cups of water. A few of the people in the park shouted for him to get back in the race.

Garry still was amazed that nobody had passed, but

finally Ian Thompson appeared. Garry decided to try and get a ride back to the finish and left the bench to ask a policeman: "Where's the meat wagon?"

The policeman looked at Garry as though he did not know what he meant. Gary tried to explain: "Can I get a police car to take me back to the finish line?"

The policeman shook his head. "How about a bus?" asked Garry.

"No."

"Subway?"

"Boy, if you want to get to the finish line, you're going to have to hoof it."

Garry began to run again. By this time nearly a hundred runners had passed. They came in clusters now, every few seconds. One of those was Barry Brown, who having gone twenty miles decided he might as well keep going. He came up to Garry Bjorklund and asked: "What happened to you?" Garry muttered something under his breath, and the two started to run together.

Also running slowly at this point was the Colombian, Victor Mora. Having run in the Pan American Games two times, Garry knew a few words of Spanish. "Caliente," he commented to Mora (meaning warm).

"Uhhhh," said Mora and quit.

Bill Rodgers was not feeling too good in the late stages of the New York City Marathon either. "The real question in my mind was whether I had anything left," he said later. When I pulled away from Garry at the Queensboro Bridge, I knew he was done. But I wasn't sure where anybody else was. I kept looking over my shoulder, but I couldn't see anyone. I just kept on running."

With about three miles to go, the course reached the northeast edge of Central Park. It followed Fifth Avenue for several blocks, then turned into the park itself,

128

where the runners encountered a series of hills. The hills were gentle enough—unless you were in the 24th mile of a 26-mile race. Bill's pace had slowed now to 5:30 per mile and he was thirsty. He had been drinking water all along the route, but for some reason none was available at this point. He yelled out to people standing by the road, but nobody had any water to offer. "I would have stopped if necessary," he said. He knew he had a lead and felt confident nobody could catch him.

Bill Rodgers crossed the finish line of the New York City Marathon in 2:12:11.6, nearly a half mile ahead of Ian Thompson, who ran 2:14:12. Then came Trevor Wright (2:14:35), Marco Marchei of Italy (2:16:54), Tom Antczak of Wisconsin (2:17:11), and Jack Foster of New Zealand (2:17:28). Foster was forty-six years old and thus won the "masters" division for runners over forty.

Frank Shorter placed 12th with 2:19:32 and seemed exultant afterward. He had run the second half of the race faster than the first and covered the last half dozen miles at better than 5:00 pace. Don Kardong struggled in 49th place with 2:26:04.

Garry Bjorklund almost stopped when he passed the New York Athletic Club with a half mile to go, "then I thought I've never dropped out of a marathon, so there was no sense starting now." His time of 2:29:58 earned him 76th place.

Only a few minutes after Garry crossed the line and walked through the chute that guided him and other finishers into a waiting area in the park, Grete Waitz of Norway appeared. Her winning time of 2:32:29.8 bettered the 2:34:48 world record held by Christa Vahlensieck of West Germany. Vahlensieck that day dropped out of the race at 18 miles with severe pain in her legs. Julie Brown, the American marathon record holder, had to stop around 22 miles when her knee locked.

Marty Cooksey had problems in the last mile. The course exited Central Park at this point and followed Fifty-ninth Street, re-entering the park at Columbus Circle. Then, with only a quarter mile to go, runners had to cross a strip of grass before reaching the last straightaway, which was slightly uphill.

Marty seemed to have no strength left. She fell down. One of the spectators tried to assist her, but she said: "No, you can't help me." Another runner helped her up and she began to run. She lunged at the finish line, but went down failing to cross it. "I crawled across the line," said Marty. Her second-place time was 2:41:48, but as the first American she was declared the National AAU champion. Medical personnel took her to the first-aid area, but after lying down for ten minutes she felt better and got up.

As Bill Rodgers and Grete Waitz talked to the press, runners continued to stream across the line and into the finishing chute to have their time and place recorded. They may have suffered pain along the way, but most had smiles on their face. Many would still be finishing hours later, long after Bill and Grete had changed. Despite the warm weather, many of these runners would set personal records* or finish a marathon for the first time. Their victory would be just as sweet as the ones won by Bill and Grete. They are marathoners too.

---

*Author Hal Higdon also competed in the New York City Marathon this day. He placed 78th with a time of 2:30:26, which set an American age-group record for forty-seven-year-olds.

AUTHOR'S NOTE

On Patriot's Day in 1979, Bill Rodgers won his third Boston Marathon in an American record performance. His winning time of 2:09:27 was 28 seconds under the American record he set in the 1975 Boston Marathon.

In the New City Marathon on October 21, 1979, Bill Rodgers and Grete Waitz duplicated their winning performances of the previous year. Rodgers' time of 2:11:42 gave him his fourth consecutive New York title. Ms. Waitz became the first woman to run a marathon in under 2 hours and 30 minutes, setting a new women's world record time of 2:27:33.

Bill Rodgers' victories at the 1979 Boston and New York marathons have confirmed his position as America's top marathoner. Ironically, while Grete Waitz would have been considered a marathon favorite in the 1980 Olympics, she will not compete because the Olympic Committee has not yet allowed an event longer than 1500 meters for women in the Olympics.

THE GREAT MARATHONERS

Over the years many great runners have left their own special print on the marathon event. Some of them were Olympic champions, some not.

PHEIDIPPIDES

The first marathoner supposedly was a Greek runner-messenger named Pheidippides (sometimes spelled Philippides), who lived nearly 2,500 years ago. His run in 490 B.C. from the plains of Marathon to the city of Athens, however, may owe as much to legend as it does to truth.

In 490 B.C. Persian soldiers invaded Greece and encountered an Athenian army commanded by Miltiades. Though outnumbered, the Greeks had armor to protect themselves against Persian swords. They also were in better shape, running being both an important sport and an important form of military training in Greece.

The Greeks charged the Persians. According to the historian Herodotus, the Greeks only lost 192 men compared to 6,400 for the defeated Persians.

Legend has it that Miltiades then dispatched Pheidippides to run to Athens, a distance of around 22 miles, to relay news of the great victory. Pheidippides supposedly ran at great speed, arrived in the city, shouted,

132

"Rejoice, we conquer!"—then dropped dead.

Historians differ on whether or not Pheidippides made such a run or, if there were such a runner, he died from the effort.

Herodotus lived at the time of the battle and he mentioned Pheidippides as the messenger dispatched by Miltiades, not to Athens after the battle, but to Sparta before it. Knowing the Athenian army was outnumbered, the Greek commander wanted the Spartans to come fight with his army.

When Pheidippides returned from his 150-mile round-trip journey, he reported that the Spartans would come, but only after the moon was full and they completed their religious ceremonies. The Spartans later fulfilled their promise, but by then the battle was over.

Herodotus mentions no messenger running to Athens, though Miltiades and his men marched there after their victory. When the Persian fleet appeared and discovered the city guarded, they headed home.

Centuries after the battle, the Roman historian Plutarch wrote about a heroic soldier running to Athens with news of the victory at Marathon. Plutarch credited the run to a warrior named Eucles. Other historians named the runner as Thersippus, but one other Roman, Lucian, spoke of him as Philippides. Perhaps he confused him with the messenger sent to Sparta.

Legend or not, the story of Pheidippides inspired a French scholar, Michel Breal, to invent the marathon before the first modern Olympic Games. In 1894 he announced a trophy for the winner of an Olympic long-distance race that would be called the marathon. Two years later, the organizers of the Olympic Games staged the first marathon. The course ran from Marathon to Athens, the same route Pheidippides might have taken centuries before.

SPIRIDON LOUES

Twenty-four centuries after the legendary run of Pheidippides, another Greek made marathon history. Spiridon Loues, a slender 25-year-old shepherd, won the marathon at the first modern Olympic Games in Athens in 1896.

Like Pheidippides, Loues had been a soldier. His former commanding officer, recalling the stamina Loues displayed during long marches, persuaded him to enter the marathon.

Quiet and determined, Loues trained by running in the hills where he tended his flocks. He fasted the day before the race and spent much of the evening in prayer.

On race day, 150,000 spectators lined the road from Marathon to Athens. Another 70,000 filled the stadium. Since no Greek athlete had yet won a gold medal in the Olympics and the marathon was the last event, the Greek spectators wanted a victory.

They offered rich prizes to the winner—should he be Greek. A tailor promised free clothing for the rest of the winner's life. A barber offered free haircuts for life. A candy maker pledged 2,000 pounds of chocolates. One wealthy man promised the hand of his daughter in marriage, along with a rich dowry.

A Greek Army colonel fired the starting gun at 2:00 P.M., and 25 runners started the rugged 40-kilometer course. Albin Lermusiaux, a Frenchman, took the lead. Thirty minutes later he passed through the village of Pikarni nearly a mile ahead of Edwin Flack, an Australian. Next came American Arthur Blake, a mile runner, and Hungarian Gyula Kellner. Spiridon Loues held fifth place.

The Pikarni villagers told Loues he was far behind. "Never mind," he replied, "I will overtake them and beat them all."

134

Blake quit just beyond the halfway mark.

Six miles from Athens, Lermusiaux held such a lead the villagers of Kavarti tried to crown him with a victory wreath. The Frenchman declined, knowing the worst part of the race was yet to come.

The course went uphill beyond Kavarti, and Lermusiaux slowed to a walk. Flack took the lead, followed by Loues. Soon afterward Lermusiaux dropped out.

Loues maintained his steady pace and soon caught Flack. The Greek ran with the Australian for about a mile, then spurted ahead. Flack faltered, stumbled, and soon collapsed.

Riders on horseback brought news to the stadium that Loues was almost a mile ahead, with two miles to go. As he neared the stadium, the crowd could hear the cheers of spectators outside.

Princes George and Constantine left the royal box to meet Loues at the stadium entrance. They jogged along with him for the last lap. After he crossed the finish line in 2:58:59, the Princes escorted him to the king to receive royal congratulations.

The spectators showered the little shepherd with both applause and gifts. Some threw him jewelry and gold watches. The tailor, the barber, and the candy maker kept their promises to reward him. Already married, Loues declined the offer of marriage to the philanthropist's daughter.

TOM LONGBOAT

At the Boston Marathon in 1907, the lead pack of runners approached a railroad crossing. Suddenly a freight train approached the same crossing in Framingham about five miles into the race.

The leaders sprinted, but only seven managed to beat the train. The rest had to stand and wait for two minutes.

135

Sixth among the swift seven was Tom Longboat, a 19-year-old Onondaga Indian from Hamilton, Ontario. Tall and silent, Longboat waited until ten miles before moving up. By the halfway point at Wellesley, he was running second.

Sleet and rain pummeled the runners, but it failed to bother Longboat. He caught Bostonian James Lee and took the lead at 17 miles. Rink Patch, another Canadian, challenged the young Indian on the Newton hills, but soon faded. Longboat pulled away, finishing in a record time of 2:24:24 for the 24.5-mile course.

Bob Fowler finished three and a half minutes later. He had been among the runners delayed by the train.

Longboat's performance may have been one of the best ever on the dusty, partly gravel, old course. Years later, Clarence DeMar said that if Longboat had run under the much improved running conditions of DeMar's day, he might have run 2:06 for the 24.5-mile distance. That would have been 15 minutes faster than the record DeMar set in 1922.

Longboat turned pro after his victory. He never ran at Boston again.

JOHNNY HAYES

The course for the 1908 Olympic marathon measured 26 miles 385 yards, the distance that later became the world standard. The British Olympic Committee wanted to let the King's grandchildren watch the start from Windsor Castle, which was exactly that far from the finish at the Olympic stadium.

Fifty-six runners started the race, including 1908 Boston Marathon winner Thomas P. Morrissey. Among those given only slim chances of winning were Johnny Hayes of the United States and Dorando Pietri of Italy.

Hayes was a small runner, 5 feet 4 inches tall and
136

weighing 126 pounds. He had short legs, but full of confidence, he liked to quote Abraham Lincoln that the ideal length of a soldier's legs was "exactly long enough to reach from his hips to the ground."

Hayes and Pietri started the London marathon slowly. Halfway through the race Charles Hefferon of South Africa had the lead. Pietri was catching the second-place runner, and Hayes lagged about a mile behind.

Then Hayes began to speed up. Mike Ryan, an American who had been trotting along with Hayes, said, "You're going too fast, Johnny."

"No, we've got to move now," Hayes replied. "Stick with me." But Ryan fell back and eventually quit.

With six miles to go, Pietri began to whittle away Hefferon's four-minute lead. The Italian sprinted past the tiring South African at 22 miles. Fearful of a challenge from Hefferon, Pietri maintained his fast pace.

Hayes overtook Hefferon as they approached the stadium. His chances of winning seemed remote since Pietri had already entered the stadium. Then Pietri's struggle began. When he arrived on the track he turned the wrong way. He looked dazed.

Officials swarmed around him, begging the Italian to turn around. Pietri pivoted, then collapsed.

The officials lifted him and shoved him toward the finish. Pietri tottered and weaved. He fell again, got up, and fell twice more. Finally, two officials dragged Pietri across the finish line and rushed him to a hospital.

Despite his courage, Pietri did not win a medal. Olympic rules forbid a runner from receiving assistance. Hayes, who finished a half minute behind Pietri, was declared the winner. Hayes was the last American to win the marathon until Frank Shorter in 1972.

The drama of Pietri's finish caused widespread public concern that the marathon was too dangerous.

137

Some doctors claimed it should be banned from future Olympics.

But the drama also stimulated great interest in marathon running in America. Both Hayes and Pietri turned professional and faced each other in a match race in New York. Pietri avenged his defeat in London by beating Hayes by 60 yards.

HANNES KOLEHMAINEN

Only two countries have won as many gold medals as the United States in men's track and field during a single Olympic Games. One country is the Soviet Union. The other is Finland, a nation half the size of Texas.

In 1920 a handful of Finns won eight gold medals, tying a much larger American team. The eighth gold medalist on the Finnish team was Hannes Kolehmainen, winner of the marathon.

Kolehmainen was well-known because of his exploits at the 1912 Olympics in Stockholm. He won the 5,000 meters, the 10,000 meters, and the 8,000-meter cross-country. Later he set world records in distances ranging from 3,000 meters to 30 kilometers. Because of World War I, the 1916 Olympics were never held, otherwise Hannes might have won more medals.

A tall, slim runner with a smooth, effortless stride, Kolehmainen came from a running family. His brother Willie toured the United States in 1910 as a professional distance runner. Another brother, Tatu, ran in the Olympic 10,000 meters and marathon in Stockholm.

But Hannes was the most gifted of the three. In the 5,000 meters at Stockholm he sprinted the last 50 meters to defeat Frenchman Jean Brouin by a step. Both men broke the world record by more than 20 seconds. In the 10,000 meters, Kolehmainen led from start to finish,

138

beating runner-up Lewis Tewanima of the United States by more than 45 seconds.

Kolehmainen's Stockholm victories inspired many young Finns to train for distance running, including Paavo Nurmi, Ville Ritola, and Albin Stenroos, all gold medalists in the 1920s. Sportswriters dubbed the Finnish runners "The Flying Finns," and Hannes Kolehmainen was the first of them.

After the 1912 Olympics, Hannes accepted an invitation to compete in the United States. The Finn ran in American championships and eventually married an American woman. But Kolehmainen wore his national colors for the 1920 Olympic marathon in Antwerp, Belgium.

Thirty runners started the race, following flat stone roads to and from the outlying village of Runspi. A Belgian took an early lead, but soon yielded to Christopher Gitsham of South Africa, silver medalist in the 1912 Olympic marathon. Kolehmainen trailed Gitsham, content to let the South African set the pace.

Just after turning at Runspi, a young Estonian, Juri Lossman, took the lead. Kolehmainen accelerated to keep up and passed Gitsham, whose leg was hurting from a previous injury. Gitsham eventually dropped out.

Several miles later Kolehmainen passed Lossman. Although the Estonian tried to match Kolehmainen surges, he could not regain the lead.

Kolehmainen finished in 2:32:35.8, fifty yards ahead of Lossman. The victory overjoyed Finnish spectators, who wrapped Kolehmainen in a Finnish flag, crowned him with laurels, and forced him to run a victory lap. Ironically, their tribute almost caused the weary Kolehmainen to collapse.

Officials later discovered that the Belgian course

was more than 26.5 miles, giving Kolehmainen the added distinction of winning the longest marathon in Olympic history.

CLARENCE DEMAR

What A. J. Foyt is to auto racing, Clarence H. DeMar is to marathoning. He won the Boston Marathon seven times, a record that probably will stand forever. At the peak of his running career, DeMar won three years in a row.

Marathoning was serious business to DeMar, just as his life had been. His father died when he was eight. Two years later his mother placed Clarence in a state vocational school because she could not afford to support her six children.

DeMar studied hard and graduated first in his class. He also began running and writing magazine stories, often about the marathon. After graduation he worked as a printer for Boston newspapers, then started his own printing business in Melrose, Massachusetts.

Clarence's doctor warned him not to run the Boston Marathon because of a heart murmur. But DeMar ran anyway and finished in record time, capturing his first victory at age twenty.

Afterward DeMar took his doctor's advice and withdrew from the sport for several years. But he felt frustrated watching from the sidelines. In spite of the supposed risk, he started running again in 1917.

It turned out that the doctor had made a poor diagnosis. DeMar did not have a heart murmur. At the end of his career at age sixty-five, DeMar had a complete physical examination, and the examiners found his heart to be in perfect condition.

DeMar began his string of three consecutive wins in 1922. That year he battled James Henigan of Medford, Massachusetts, for 13 miles. Then DeMar surged ahead at

140

the 20-mile point. He finished in 2:18:10, an all-time record for the old 24.5-mile course.

Next year DeMar followed Whitey Michelson through the Newton hills between 17 and 20 miles. He caught Michelson at Cleveland Circle, about four miles from the finish, and went on to win.

In 1924 DeMar dominated the entire race. He led at the halfway mark, built up a 500-yard lead over the hills, and finished more than five minutes ahead of the next runner.

DeMar's time of 2:29:40 became a new mark to beat, since the course had been lengthened to the Olympic distance of 26 miles 385 yards. (Actually the 1924 course was 176 yards short. It was extended in 1927.)

DeMar won again in 1927, 1928, and 1930. Sportswriters said the race should be renamed "DeMarathon."

A solitary person, DeMar trained alone, strived for excellence, and disliked anyone who got in his way. He once punched a fan who tried to get his autograph during the race. Another spectator tried to help DeMar stay cool by splashing him with a dipper of water. DeMar punched him too.

Clarence also disliked the hoopla at the finish line. He had no use for the reporters, photographers, city officials, and well-wishers who swarmed around him. DeMar once commented he preferred to finish behind the leaders to avoid the commotion.

DeMar ran the Boston Marathon until he was sixty-three. He finished in the top ten 15 times, including a remarkable seventh place at age fifty. He died of cancer in 1958 at the age of seventy. Despite what doctors had earlier said, nothing had been wrong with his heart.

EMIL ZATOPEK

Spectators at the 1952 Olympics in Helsinki, Finland, were used to great distance-running feats. Their countrymen, Kolehmainen, Nurmi, Ritola and other "Flying Finns," had set new standards of running excellence. Yet the Finns were stunned when Emil Zatopek of Czechoslovakia announced he would enter the marathon after winning the 5,000 and 10,000 meters. No one before had ever attempted such a daring triple.

Zatopek had never even run a 26-mile race, and few observers gave him much chance over the experienced marathoners. Yet the bold attempt was characteristic of Zatopek, then a twenty-eight-year-old captain in the Czechoslovakian army.

Zatopek became serious about running at age eighteen. He placed second in his first race, just two seconds behind his trainer. From then on, Zatopek began seeking races with tougher competition. He frequently lost, but his times improved rapidly.

Zatopek joined the army during World War II. Afterward he went to the military academy for officer's training. The Czech ran constantly. He strove to increase his speed with interval training, running many short distances at top speed. During the winter he trudged through snow and ice, training in combat boots. Sometimes, training at night, he carried a flashlight to see his way.

The training paid off. Zatopek was undefeated at 5,000 meters in 1947, ranking number one in the world. He won the 10,000 meters at the 1948 Olympics in London, placing second at the shorter distance. In 1949 he broke the world record twice in the 10,000 meters.

It was not only Zatopek's speed that amazed the sporting world. It was his form. Short and wiry, he seemed to run in agony. His head wobbled. His face grimaced in pain. He puffed and groaned loudly. One sportswriter said: "He runs like a man who has just been stabbed in the heart."

142

But these bizarre contortions belied Zatopek's superb condition. His short, smooth stride never varied. He ran at a murderous pace, and his reserves of energy seemed limitless.

After only three days rest following his 5,000 victory at Helsinki, Zatopek lined up with 66 other runners for the start of the marathon. Jim Peters of Britain led out of the stadium. Zatopek stayed back, content to follow.

Near the halfway mark, he caught Peters. The Czech, speaking English, asked the British runner if the pace was fast enough. Peters, exhausted already, said it was too slow. Amazed, Zatopek said, "You say 'too slow'? Are you sure the pace is too slow?"

"Yes," answered Peters. Zatopek shrugged and started running faster.

Zatopek and Gustaf Jansson of Sweden reached the turnaround together, with Peters falling behind. A breeze blew into their faces, and running became harder.

Zatopek had a small lead when the Swede stopped for fruit juice. Seeing his chance to break away, Zatopek galloped over two hills. Then he looked back. To his relief, he saw Jansson had fallen far behind.

Alone, Zatopek was moving along at a phenomenal speed. He passed the three-quarters mark 12 seconds ahead of world-record pace. His legs ached and his feet began to blister, but he held the pace.

Zatopek entered the stadium a half-mile ahead of his nearest rival. The crowd went wild, chanting, "Zat-o-pek, Zat-o-pek, Zat-o-pek." He wearily pushed himself around the last lap and broke the tape with uplifted arms. He smiled. He had won the 5,000 meters, the 10,000 meters, and the marathon, a triple victory that would stand out forever in Olympic history. In addition, his marathon time of 2:23:3.2 was more than six minutes faster than the Olympic record.

Zatopek seemed to recover from his effort in minutes. He was munching on an apple and greeting friends when the next runner entered the stadium. He later commented to a reporter: "The marathon is a very boring race."

Zatopek had earned a well-deserved rest, but later that year he demolished four world records in a single run. En route to the record at 30 kilometers, he broke records for the one-hour run, 15 miles, and 25 kilometers. Zatopek then held every official world record from 10,000 meters up.

ABEBE BIKILA

The city of Rome offered a superb setting for the 1960 Olympic marathon. The course started at the foot of Capitol Hill, the center of the ancient Roman Empire. It wound out and around the city. The final miles followed the Appian Way, a cobblestoned road built in 300 B.C.

A sunset start added to the spectacle. The runners finished by moonlight and in the glare of torches.

The pageantry in itself would have made the event memorable. But a slender Ethiopian soldier made it even more so. Running barefoot, Abebe Bikila strode down the torchlit Appian Way ahead of 69 other runners.

Bikila was a palace guard of Emperor Haile Selassie of Ethiopia. He held back early in the race. Near the halfway point he joined the leaders, then broke away from the pack along with Moroccan, Rhadi Ben Abdesselam. With less than a mile to go, the Moroccan tried to move ahead, but Bikila responded with an even faster sprint. Bikila finished well ahead with a time of 2:15:16.2, faster than anyone before had run the marathon distance.

Four years later in Tokyo, Bikila took an early lead. He never lost it and finished four minutes ahead of the next runner, running 2:12:11.2. Seemingly unaffected by
144

fatigue, he lay down on the grassy infield and performed some brisk calisthenics.

Many spectators thought he was showing off. But Bikila was doing what he always did after a hard workout. He exercised to avoid cramps.

Bikila made a great impression on the world of sports by his graceful and apparently effortless running. But few people knew him well. He was detached and remote, almost to the point of aloofness. Although Bikila knew some English, he preferred to speak in his native Amharic.

Bikila shunned strangers. He rarely gave interviews. Even in Ethiopia, where he was a national hero, he avoided public places. Bikila would run, perform his duties as sports instructor in the Imperial Bodyguard, and spend time with his family of three sons and one daughter.

Bikila loved to run. According to one story, he would chase pheasants until they fell from fatigue. He trained under a Swedish coach, Onni Niskanen, and often practiced by running fast, then slow, then fast without stopping. This built Bikila's stamina and speed.

Bikila's confidence was unshakable. Although practically an unknown at the time, he predicted his victory at Rome. His chances at Tokyo seemed no better, since he had an appendix operation 40 days before the race. But he again predicted his victory, and won.

Bikila predicted a third win at Mexico City in 1968. His chances seemed excellent, since he trained in the 7,000-foot-high mountains of Ethiopia. The elevation of Mexico City was about the same. But the Ethiopian suffered an ankle injury that forced him to drop out of the race, and his fellow countryman Mamo Wolde placed first, making it three marathon gold medals in a row for Ethiopia.

Bikila's running career came to a tragic end in 1969 when an automobile accident left him paralyzed from the waist down. He spent the rest of his life in a wheelchair and died at age 47.

Bikila accepted his fate with the same quiet strength he showed as a marathon champion. Several years before his death in 1973 the brave Ethiopian said in a *Sports Illustrated* interview, "It was the will of God that I won the Olympics, and it was the will of God that I had my accident. I was overjoyed when I won the marathon twice. But I accepted those victories as I accept this tragedy. I have no choice. I have to accept both circumstances as facts of life and live happily."

JOHN A. KELLEY

The timers at the Boston Marathon stop recording runners after three-and-a-half hours. That has been the official cut-off point since 1977. But for millions of spectators who line the course and jam the finish at the Prudential Center, the race is not over until 71-year-old Johnny A. Kelley crosses the line.

More than any other runner Johnny Kelley (the Elder) symbolizes the spirit of the Boston Marathon. The knobby-kneed veteran will not quit. As of 1978 he had run the race 48 times, more than anyone else in history.

The fans love Kelley. They cheer him and throw kisses, just as they did Clarence DeMar several decades before. Parents point him out to their children. And Kelley loves the fans. He waves back at them. Tears come to his sparkling green eyes. "You can't help it out there," he says. "The people are all so beautiful."

But the spectators did not always have long to wait for Johnny to finish. He won the Boston Marathon two times.

Raised in Arlington, Massachusetts, Kelley started

146

running at age 12 after seeing his first marathon. He worked part-time at a gas station, and he trained during his dinner hour.

Kelley entered the race in 1928 at age 17. He dropped out with bloody and blistered feet at 17 miles. Six years later Kelley took second. They next year, in 1935, he won.

Kelley, then a florist's assistant, won that marathon race with ease. For the first 13 miles Kelley dueled with Dave Komonen, a cobbler from Ontario who had defeated Kelley the year before. Then Komonen dropped out. Kelley ran the rest of the way unchallenged.

In 1945 he ran cautiously, trailing the lead pack by 750 yards at the halfway mark. He passed three runners on the hills and chased after leader Lloyd Bairstow. He finally overtook Bairstow three miles from the finish and won with a two-minute margin.

Besides running at Boston, Kelley competed in the 1936 and 1948 Olympic marathons.

Retired and living on Cape Cod in Massachusetts, Kelley runs five to ten miles every day and also does oil paintings, which he sells. He finished the 1978 Boston Marathon in 3:32, saying: "My heart belongs to Boston."

JOHN J. KELLEY

Foreign runners won the Boston Marathon for eleven consecutive years after Johnny Kelley's 1945 victory. Then in 1957 a Connecticut schoolteacher sped to an impressive victory. His name also was Johnny Kelley.

John J. Kelley, no relation to the 1945 winner, breezed by three Japanese, two Finns, three Koreans, a Mexican, several Canadians and all other Americans. Only the 1954 winner, Veikko Karvonen, stayed close, but John left him at 16 miles.

They called him Young John, or Kelley the

Younger, to distinguish him from Old John. In the 1957 race he beat Karvonen by nearly three-fourths of a mile, establishing a course record of 2:20:05.

Not only was Young John the first American in eleven years to win at Boston, he also was the first winner who belonged to the Boston Athletic Association, the organization that founded the race in 1897. B.A.A. President Walter A. Brown was so proud he presented Kelley with a gold watch in addition to the diamond medal given each winner.

In 1958 Kelley placed second. Second place slot seemed to have a hold on the Kelleys. Young John finished second five times in his Boston career, with Old John taking seven seconds.

Following Kelley's 1957 win, foreign runners re-established their domination of the race. But Kelley again played a part in breaking a long string of foreign victories. He coached the next American winner, Ambrose Burfoot, a student from Wesleyan University who won in 1968. And Burfoot roomed with and helped inspire Bill Rodgers, who would win at Boston in 1975, 1978, and 1979.

THE GREAT MARATHONS OF THE WORLD

Marathons are held on all continents of the world.

Some of them are big, such as New York; some are small, such as the Heart of America Marathon in Columbia, Missouri. Some are limited, such as the Olympic Marathon, which permits only three entries per country.

Most world-class marathoners look to the Olympic Marathon each four years as the number-one race. Boston and Fukuoka have similar status as elite runs, because of the fast fields they attract. Other runners may be attracted to lesser-known events such as the Avenue of the Giants Marathon, run beneath giant redwood trees in California, or the Sea of Galilee Marathon, run entirely below sea level and through kibbutzim in Israel.

Here are some of the marathons that have the most appeal to runners:

BOSTON

The oldest annual marathon in the world, started in 1897 by members of the Boston Athletic Association after they saw the first Olympic Marathon in Athens the year before. Tradition makes this the goal of most American runners and attracts top foreigners as well. In addition, a million or more spectators line the course to cheer the marathoners as they pass. The race is held on Patriot's Day, the third Monday in April, a holiday in most of New England. To gain entry, runners must have bettered time standards: 2:50 for men, 3:20 for women and 3:10 for men over age 40. More than 8,000 official entrants started the Boston Marathon in 1979, with maybe another 3,000 unofficial runners starting without numbers.

OLYMPICS

This marathon race predates Boston by one year (1896), but is held only every fourth year during the Olympic Games and in whichever city the games are held. Each country can enter only their top three marathoners, which causes intense competition in different countries to be part of the Olympic team. In the United States every fourth year, the Olympic trial marathon usually becomes the year's fastest race. Buffalo, New York; Eugene, Oregon (twice); and Alamosa, Colorado, have served as sites for recent American trial races. The winner of the Olympic gold medal in the marathon earns respect as the best long-distance runner—for four years.

NEW YORK

In 1897 a marathon from Stamford, Connecticut, to New York finished in Columbus Circle, next to Central Park, but it did not survive. For years, the National AAU utilized a rugged, hilly course in suburban Yonkers for its national championship marathon. Other races within New York City used various courses, including one in Central Park, beginning in 1970, that attracted 126 finishers. Then in 1976 New Yorkers moved the start of their race to Staten Island, on the approach to the Verrazano-Narrows Bridge, and ran through all five boroughs before finishing in Central Park. The uniqueness of this inner-city run attracted nearly 10,000 starters in 1978 and

150

maybe as many spectators as Boston. Almost overnight, the New York City Marathon became one of the great races of the world.

HONOLULU

Another race with a short history, the Honolulu Marathon was started in 1973 and attracted only 162 runners, almost all of them from the Islands. By 1978, the event attracted 7,111 entrants, 1,412 of them female. Most of them were lured by the appeal of the Hawaiian Islands, good race organization, and the hospitality of the organizers. "It's not a fast marathon," claims Jeff Wells, the 1977 winner, "but it's probably the most enjoyable to run." Runners start at 6:00 A.M. to avoid the heat and humidity present even in early December in the tropics. The Honolulu Marathon does not end even when the last finisher crosses the line eight hours later. Picnics continue in Kapiolani Park into late afternoon.

PIKES PEAK

Not really a "marathon," even though the round-trip distance up and down Pikes Peak covers 28.1 miles. The Pikes Peak Marathon, held each August, is more a mountain climb. Runners start in Manitou Springs near the 7000-foot level and wind their way up Bair Trail to the summit of the 14,110-foot mountain first discovered by Lieutenant Zebulon Montgomery Pike in 1806. Most entrants stop at the summit and ride back down, but other competitors turn and run all the way. "I run it for the challenge of man against nature," says Ken Young, winner at Pikes Peak in 1978. Because of crowding on the narrow trails, this race is now limited to only 750 entrants.

POLYTECHNIC

Great Britain has many marathons, but they attract smaller fields and are less "people's events" than most present-day American races. Among the best English marathons is the "Poly," run over part of the 1908 Olympic course that first established 26 miles 385 yards as the official marathon distance. That race started near Windsor Castle and finished in White City Stadium. After 1908, the Poly Marathon continued each year, starting at Windsor Castle and finishing at Stamford Bridge, later at Chiswick Stadium, most recently at Windsor Track.

COMRADES
This South African race is 56 miles long, thus is considered an *ultra*-marathon rather than a standard marathon. It was started in 1921 by a group of World War I veterans in memory of their dead comrades. In alternate years, the race follows the "up" course from Durban to Pietermaritzburg or the "down" course the other direction. Either way, Comrades is one of the most difficult mass races in the world, not only because of the distance, but because of long and steep hills. Nevertheless, in 1979, of 3001 starters, 2824 finished the race under the eleven-hour standard, a finishing rate of 94.1 percent.

FUKUOKA
This Japanese race ranks high in prestige among world-class marathoners because its sponsors bring in the fastest runners in the world, who compete over a flat and fast, out-and-back course. Crowds equal to those in Boston or New York cheer the runners, who must have run times faster than 2:30 to enter. Because of the quality of the field and because the race in this western Japanese city of four million people occurs in December, the Fukuoka Marathon sometimes is considered the unofficial world-championship marathon race.

Other prestige races that attract quality fields to fast
152

courses include the Nike/Oregon Track Club race in Eugene in September and the Kosice Marathon in Czechoslovakia in October.

INDEX

Page numbers in italics refer to photographs.

154

New York City Marathon, 71, 72,
 75, 78, 79, 80-81, 82, 83, 84,
 88, 108, 110-30, 149, 150-51
 biggest running event in world,
 114
 budget, 113, 119
 course, 114, 115
 dual starting line, 118
 first, 112
 history, 150
 1978 winners, 129
 number of runners, 115
 percent who finish, 117
 sponsorship. *See* Manufacturers
 Hanover Trust Company
New York Road Runners Club,
 111, 112, 114
New Zealand Marathon, 110
Nike, 49
Nike/Oregon Track Club race, 153
Niskanen, Onni, 145
Nurmi, Paavlo, 139, 142

Olinek, Gayle, 86
Olympic awards, 34
 ancient, 134
 See also Gold Medals, Olympic;
 Silver Medals, Olympic
Olympic cities. *See* Olympic Games
Olympic Games
 first marathon, 133, 134
 first modern. *See* Olympic Games,
 1896
 history of marathon, 132, 147,
 149, 150
 1896 (Greece), 10, 45, 133, 134
 1900 (Paris), 10
 1904 (St. Louis), 10
 1908 (London), 10-11, 53, 136
 1912 (Stockholm), 11, 138-40
 1916 (canceled), 138
 1920 (Antwerp), 11, 138, 139
 1924 (Paris), 11
 1936 (Berlin), 147

1948 (London), 142, 147
1952 (Helsinki), 11, 141, 143
1956 (Cortina), 14
1960 (Rome), 11, 144
1964 (Tokyo), 11, 12, 144-45
1968 (Mexico), 12, 13, 26, 145
1972 (Munich), 10, 12, 17, 19, 21,
 98, 99
1976 (Montreal), 88, 117, 123
1980 (Moscow), 108, 131
See also gold medals, Olympic;
 silver medals, Olympic
Olympic records, 9, 35
 triple (5,000-, and 10,000-meter
 marathons), 143
Olympic rules, 10, 137
 restrict women, 131
Olympic trials, marathon. *See* Marathons
Olympics
 number of contestants, 106
 training, 102
O'Rourke, Frank, 38

Pan American Games, 12, 98, 103,
 128
Parker, John, 23
Patch, Rink, 136
Patriot's Day, 44, 131, 149
Peach Bowl Marathon, 70, 71
Peachtree Race, 69
Perillat, Guy, 14
Peters, Jim, 143
Pheidippides, 10, 11, 132-33, 134
Pietri, Dorando, 10, 53, 136, 137,
 138
 sets official Marathon distance,
 11
Pike, Lt. Zebulon Montgomery, 151
Pikes Peak Marathon, 151
Polytechnic Marathon, 151-52
Prefontaine, Steve, 97, 98
Puma, 49
Puttemans, Emil, 106, 107

158